Praise For *The Dialogue*

"The Dialogue touched me very deeply. It's a small but extremely useful handbook to higher consciousness, told through a conversation between a wise elder and a young seeker. What surprised me about the book was how elegantly it approached one of the crucial problems of our time—the integration of science and spirit. Jim Cusumano is an ideal vehicle for the transmission of these ideas. I've had occasion to meet him at various times over the past fifteen years and have found him to be a most rare combination of clear-eyed scientist and open-hearted mystic. The Dialogue will inspire you, as it inspired me, and at the same time open your eyes to a new way of seeing the world."

—Gay Hendricks, Ph.D.
Author of *The Big Leap* and *The Corporate Mystic*
President, The Hendricks Institute
Ojai, California

"A small but important book, its pages densely packed with the greatest questions we can ask and the likely, truly plausible answers or counter-questions we can envisage . . . A wonderful read for a quiet weekend, or a moment's contemplation of the mysteries of the universe that are not only outside us, but actually and truly within us."

"*The Dialogue* is an excellent guide to insights gleaned from the world's wisdom traditions."

"I started to skim Jim Cusumano's book, *The Dialogue,* but it drew me in so intensely. I devoured the whole thing in one go. Brilliant, informative, entertaining, and a masterclass on the meaning of life".

THE DIALOGUE

"He who looks outside, dreams; he who looks within, awakens."

Carl Jung—

THE DIALOGUE

A Journey to Universal Truth

A teenage boy finds answers to life's biggest questions—

JAMES A. CUSUMANO

Waterside Productions

Waterside Productions

Printed in the United States of America

First Printing, 2020

ISBN-13: 978-1-949003-39-0 print edition
ISBN-13: 978-1-949003-40-6 ebook edition

Waterside Productions
2055 Oxford Ave
Cardiff, CA 92007
www.waterside.com

For Ricardo B. Levy

*My lifelong business partner, best friend
and spiritual beacon*

**Books by
James A. Cusumano**

Fiction

The Fallen: As Above, So Below

Twin Terror: Good Seed, Bad Seed

Non-Fiction

Freedom from Mid-East Oil
(with Coauthors Jerry B. Brown and Rinaldo S. Brutoco)

*Cosmic Consciousness:
A Journey to Well-being, Happiness and Success*

BALANCE: The Business-Life Connection

Life Is Beautiful: 12 Universal Rules

TABLE OF CONTENTS

AUTHOR'S INTRODUCTION

"Only when love and need are one,
And work is play for mortal stakes,
Is the deed ever really done
For heaven and the future's sakes."
—Robert Frost

Ever since the birth of the universe as the Big Bang, scientists have tried to explain the nature of the cosmos by searching for a way to unite the four fundamental forces of the universe—gravity, electromagnetism, the strong nuclear force, and the weak nuclear force—into one unified theory. This they said would be the ultimate theory—an intimate, workable combination of Einstein's theory of relativity and quantum physics. Their thinking has been that in doing so, they could explain all events that have ever happened or could happen, possibly even the very purpose of the universe. This undertaking they have called a quest to find the "Theory of Everything," or the TOE.

Einstein spent the last 30 years of his life unsuccessfully trying to do just that. So, you can be certain that discovering the TOE is a most difficult and monumental undertaking.

A popular approach considered by some physicists as the one that will eventually produce a workable and useful TOE, is based on what's known as "string theory."

Many outstanding theoretical physicists have spent some of their best years on this daunting pursuit, hoping it would lead to this holy grail of physics, but they have yet to come anywhere close to success.

While the string theory approach to uncovering the TOE is an exciting and noble pursuit, there are persuasive pro and con arguments offered by two camps of reputable scientists. One adamantly dismisses string theory because they maintain there is no possible way to experimentally verify the theory's validity. The other camp counters that given enough time and effort, experimental concerns and validation can be addressed.

The inadequacy of the string theory approach is supported by the fact that it predicts the existence of an unfathomable number of parallel universes—10^{500}—the number one followed by 500 zeros, each universe, independent of all the others and each having a completely different set of laws of physics than those for the other universes. To give you a sense of the unimaginable size of this number, there are approximately 10^{80} atoms in our entire observable universe. In other words, on average, the number of parallel universes predicted by string theory is 10^{420} times greater than the number of all the atoms that make up our universe—incomprehensible to say the least.

And so, parallel competing theories have tried to succeed where string theory has failed, but they too have met with minimal progress.

Although trained some years ago as a physical chemist in graduate physics, chemistry and mathematics, I don't consider myself adequately schooled and sufficiently experienced to take either side of the ensuing debate among these adept scientists. However, I think all these theories miss an important point.

As hopefully will be made apparent in this book, the true reality of our universe and all its contents are not what we perceive with our five-sense, three-dimensional, observational capabilities. True reality of all physical things, from mountains to galaxies, from microbes to men, exists only in the realm of consciousness. The physical reality we observe with our five senses is merely a mirror of that true reality, and as difficult as it may be to understand and accept, quantum physics has proven that we create our physical reality by our observation. This is the well-known Observer Effect.

As such, our current approach to uncovering the TOE will fall short of understanding the true reality of the cosmos. An analogy would be like trying to understand the workings of a laser or a microchip with classical Newtonian physics when they can only be explained by quantum physics.

If we look back in history, we can see that physics has moved circuitously in fits and starts over the last 400 years from Galilean physics to Newtonian physics to relativity and quantum physics. The next transition, I believe, will be to what some have called *spiritual physics*. This science has nothing to do with religion or theology but receives its name from the ethereal non-physical nature of phenomena which are the subject of this science. However, don't be deceived. The power of this branch of physics has much greater potential than any of the classical or quantum concepts that are the basis for its predecessor science.

To be sure, there will be dissension, argument, and debate about the legitimacy and veracity of the rules, conjectures, laws, and theorems of spiritual physics, just as there were at the transition points between the other stages of the physical sciences. We only need read but a few of the commentaries about the works of Galileo, Newton, and Planck, at the time their research results were released to the scientific community to see the resistance their ideas faced. These geniuses were, at first, considered strange prognosticators, rather than leading-edge scientists. Their discoveries were so profound that it took time for their counterintuitive findings and predicted consequences to be accepted and gain a strong foothold in the scientific world.

Even more to that point, because these new areas of physics were major leaps of thought from then current thinking, sometimes even these innovators and game-changers, at first, doubted their own findings.

For example, if you studied the early work of Nobel laureate Max Planck, who in 1900 discovered quantum physics, you would find that in order to derive the relevant equation that explained the data he and others had measured for the behavior of thermal radiant energy, a daring, seemingly illogical assumption had to be made. Planck lamented, "In a state of desperation I was forced to make a most disconcerting assumption."[1] It turned out to be *the* fundamental basis for all of quantum physics.

But that single disconcerting assumption—that all electromagnetic energy such as light or heat is not transmitted in a continuous stream as Isaac Newton and James Clerk Maxwell had maintained but moves in small discrete packets later called quanta—gave birth to quantum physics and a completely new world order.

Considered the most successful branch of science ever, quantum physics has never made an erroneous prediction and is currently responsible for practical products that make up 40 percent of our global Gross Domestic Product—lasers, microchips, cell phones, computers, photovoltaic solar cells and much, much more. This immense progress came despite uphill battles among some of the most brilliant minds at the time. For the development of spiritual physics, I believe there will also be disconcerting assumptions and the same healthy discourse and debate.

The format of this book is not unlike Galileo's famous book with a similar title.[a] Published in 1632, *The Dialogue* was conversations between three fictional characters expressing their respective views concerning the nature of the universe. *Salvati* represented Galileo's point of view—that the Earth revolved about the sun. *Simplicio* spoke to Ptolemy's view— that the sun revolved about the Earth, at the time, considered unquestionable doctrine by the Church of Rome. And *Sagrado*, a nobleman, presented his views as a layman.

In Galileo's book it was abundantly clear that he rejected the Ptolemaic Theory, namely that the sun and the heavens revolve about the Earth, but instead he embraced the Copernican Theory, which maintained that the Earth revolved around the sun. For the content of his monograph, by order of the Inquisition Court of the Church of Rome, he was sentenced to be burned at the stake like his friend and fellow scientist, Giordano Bruno. However, through the intercession of high-level friends and because he ultimately—but deceptively—recanted his views, he was saved at the very last moment from those flames, and instead spent the rest of his life under house arrest at his home, Villa Il Gioiello, in the town of Arcetri, near Florence.

While it is not my intent to be burned at the stake or spend the rest of my life under house arrest, it is my intent

---

[a] The precise title was *Dialogue Concerning the Two Chief World Systems, Ptolemaic and Copernican.*

to expose you, the reader, to some of the evolving tenets of spiritual physics and how they affect your life, and therefore, can be used to improve your state of affairs. Unlike Galileo and Copernicus, I am not the creator of these tenets. Their source is from much more capable men and women than I. However, I wish to note that I thoroughly embrace and use them to guide my thinking and my life journey.

In *The Dialogue*, there are two protagonists—Peter, a 16-year old Czech teenager, and Boda, a wise Avatar from Mesopotamia. Peter lives in Prague and is soon to graduate from high school and hopes to enter an excellent university. He aims to pursue a career in the physical sciences, and having a technical and curious predisposition, he finds it interesting to challenge himself and others for answers and opinions to some of life's great questions concerning humankind and the universe.

To contemplate these big questions, Peter often wanders the forest next to his home in the suburbs of Prague. On the first day of the dialogue, through what some might call *synchrodestiny*,[b] as Peter hikes through the forest, he meets a most unusual elderly gentleman.

Let the dialogue begin.

---

[b] Deepak Chopra defines *synchrodestiny* as harnessing the infinite power of what some call coincidence, to create what appear to be miracles. However, he notes there is no such thing as coincidence and in what looks like coincidence has specific purpose, meaning, direction and intention. Miracles do not exist. They are simply events that cannot be explained by the current state of the physical sciences. For example, the existence of an atomic particle in two places at once as well as the fact that the physical appearance of an object only occurs through observation, both were once considered either miraculous or impossible, but are now explainable by the laws of quantum physics.

DIALOGUE 1
THINK NOTHING

"Silence is a sign of great strength."
—Lao Tzu

The boy's name was Peter.

It was a stunning sunrise as he entered the edge of the forest, a half kilometer from his home in the village of Nebušice, a rural suburb of Prague. He and his parents had lived there as a convenience since he entered the International School of Prague (ISP), 10 years ago. Arguably the best private school in the Czech Republic, it was less than a five-minute bike ride from his home.

By local standards, 16-year old Peter was considered handsome—thin, a bit lanky with longish dark brown hair, large clear penetrating brown eyes and reasonably tall at 192 cm (6 foot three). Considerate but at times, he could be a bit precocious and quite tenacious, especially when seeking answers to his often-unusual questions and concerns.

ISP had been good for Peter, especially the language courses he'd taken. In addition to his native Czech, he had become fluent in English and French, and he spoke both with virtually no detectable accent. A bright student, who studied diligently for excellence, he was driven by his passionate quest for knowledge—very unusual for a 16-year old, but then again, Peter was not your usual 16-year old.

ISP had prepared him well to reach his long-time goal of admission to Harvard to study physics. He and his teachers were optimistic. Peter had taken several Advanced Placement (AP) courses in the sciences and mathematics. He enjoyed learning advanced concepts in these subjects and hoped his excellent grades would help him land admission to Harvard.

Peter was not a myopically focused science geek. A bit of a natural philosopher and a kind of alchemist, on his own he had read some of the writings of Plato, Socrates, Euclid, Copernicus, Paracelsus, Pythagoras, and Archimedes. His fellow students saw him as a bookworm and a nerd because of his passionate quest to answer what they thought were unanswerable questions. They liked and tolerated him, just the same.

But Peter wasn't a bookworm or nerd in the conventional sense. He liked sports, admittedly a distant second to his academic endeavors. He played volleyball and soccer for ISP, something he felt kept him in physical shape. As far as girls were concerned, he had several close *girl friends*, but had never had a *girlfriend.* That didn't faze him. He had enough on his plate. *Girls could wait.*

There was no doubt about Peter's IQ—it was up there with the best of them at ISP. But his EQ, emotional intelligence was a strange piece of work. Most of the time, he spoke and behaved as a typical 16-year old student. But then, suddenly, when his interest was piqued by some intellectual concept, his persona could jump nearly instantly into the behavior and conversational skill and style of a modern-day philosopher. It drove his friends crazy. *Who is this guy?*

It was late June and the school year had come to an end. Peter walked slowly and thoughtfully on his favorite hiking path in the forest. He was in one of his philosophical moods, lost in thought. *Summer is such a great time of the year in this forest. I can think clearly. I feel really good hiking here.*

Peter had walked for nearly 30 minutes, thinking about questions he had thought about many times before—*how did the universe begin? What's consciousness and where does it come from? What's the meaning and purpose of life? What's my purpose?* Tough questions—very tough.

He came to a fork in the path. He had seen this route many times before and always passed it by. It looked to him like everyone did. There were huge tall weeds growing on the path. As he stood there gazing up the steep trail, smothered in undergrowth, he thought—*Nope, I better not. I'm not in the mood to be skirting high weeds and underbrush. It'll take away from my relaxation and thoughts about things of interest to me. Who wants to be a weed dodger anyway?*

So, Peter passed by this alternate path, but about a hundred meters later, he stopped and looked back. He wasn't sure why. Suddenly and for no reason he could fathom, he recalled from last year's English lit class the first and last stanzas of Robert Frost's poem, *The Road Not Taken.*

> *Two roads diverged in a yellow wood,*
> *And sorry I could not travel both*
> *And be one traveler, long I stood*
> *And looked down as far as I could*
> *To where it bent in the undergrowth;*

* * *

I shall be telling this with a sigh
Somewhere ages and ages hence:
Two roads diverged in a wood, and I,
I took the one less traveled by,
And it made all the difference.

Peter turned around and walked back to the fork in the path. He looked up the hill and somewhat reluctantly started his trek on this new route. He didn't know why. It wasn't an easy hike, being much steeper than the path he usually took, and it was covered with high weeds which made progress slow and cumbersome. He had to walk carefully to avoid stinging nettles and his socks were increasingly covered with spiny grass burs that scratched unmercifully at his ankles. He stopped periodically to remove them. But, he persisted, wondering at times, *Was this a good idea?*

After 45 minutes or so, Peter stopped to catch his breath and rest. It was exhausting avoiding nettles, the higher weeds and those with thorns. He was nearly to the top of the incline. Wiping the sweat from his forehead with his right sleeve, he gazed towards the top. Suddenly, he saw through the bushes and trees what looked like an older man with long silver hair, sitting on a red carpet set on the ground under a tall evergreen. *What in the world?* Peter moved cautiously to the crest of the hill.

His eyes had not deceived him. An elderly man sat on a bright red carpet placed neatly under an evergreen tree. Peter stopped some distance from him to assess the situation. The man was dressed in a flowing robe of many bright colors with a gold-colored rope-belt at his waist. On his left side, there was a pair of sandals placed neatly next to the red carpet. They were very basic and appeared to have been hand-made.

The gentleman had clear dark brown skin, wore his hair in a long ponytail, held in place by a gold ring, and had plump slightly-rosy cheeks. He looked like a combination of a Middle Eastern Santa Claus and a character out of *Lawrence of Arabia*.

As he approached the man, Peter noticed the gentleman was sitting in a lotus position, his eyes closed, his hands folded as if in prayer, and his mouth curved in a slight smile, kind of like a bust of Buddha. Peter stopped directly in front of the man. The man did not move.

Old Man

Suddenly, in a humorous, slow, melodious voice, he said, "I see you."

Peter

"How can you see me? Your eyes are closed."

Old Man

In a cheerful tone, he added, "Not my third eye."

Peter

"Huh?"

Old Man

"Only kidding," he said, as he opened his eyes, which were a deep dark blue, a striking contrast to his ebony-colored skin.

Peter

"What are you doing up here?"

Old Man

"Oh, nothing really. I'm just sitting here *not* thinking or doing, just being."

Peter

"You're just being. What does that mean?"

Old Man

"Just what I said—being!"

Peter

"How often do you come up here to do your *being*?"

Old Man

Oh, every day that it doesn't rain. And when it rains, I sit in one of those hunters' blind platforms up over the hill in the farmer's field. They have nice overhangs, so I don't get wet."

Peter

"Why haven't I run into you before?"

Old Man

"Oh, that's easy. Because like everyone else, you never take this path. It's steep, overgrown, and a much more cumbersome and uncomfortable hike than the other path."

Peter

"I see."

Old Man

"Why have you taken this path today?"

Peter

"I don't know—curiosity, I guess. I always take the path down below because it's flat, no rocks, no weeds, and it's well groomed for walking and thinking."

Trying for a little humor, Peter quipped, "But I guess this is the 'no thinking, just being' path, right?"

Old Man

"I guess you could call it that. You know the act of being is important. After all, you are a human being and not a human doing. Please don't get me wrong. Doing is an important part of life. But being—that's where great things happen." He smiled.

"Take your very existence. Have you ever thought about your probability of being here at this exact moment in time?

Peter

"Not really. Should I?"

Old Man

"Absolutely! It's much more important and rewarding than you might think. Tell me, do you like math?"

Peter

"Actually, I love math."

Old Man

"Great! Then allow me to do a simple calculation for you—the probability of your being here at this very moment in time."

Peter

"Sounds interesting, but how are you going to do that?"

Old Man

"Okay; let's see, in your life, you have had two parents, four grandparents, eight grandparents—well, you get the idea, right?

Peter

"Sure."

Old Man

"Okay; this is a simple statistics and probability calculation. Suppose we go back just 30 generations to calculate your probability of being here at this very moment. Then the total number of people responsible for your being here at this time is $2 + 2^2 + 2^3 + 2^4 + \ldots 2^{30}$, which gives $2 + 4 + 8 + 16 + \ldots$, etc., all the way up to 2^{30}. You're good in math, so I'm sure you get the idea. Guess what the number is?"

Peter

"Well, it's a straightforward calculation, but I couldn't do it without a calculator. It certainly must be a very big number."

Old Man

"Right you are. The answer is 2,147,482,646 or about 2.2 billion people!"

Peter

"Are you kidding me? You couldn't do that calculation in your head."

Old Man

"Oh yes I can."

The old man pulled out a small hand calculator from his backpack and handed it to Peter, who immediately did the calculation.

Peter

"Oh my God, it's 2,147,482,646. That's amazing! How did you do that?"

Old Man

"Yes, it is amazing; not millions or hundreds of millions, but billions of people. And if one of them had been missing, died prematurely, or had not been in the right mood one evening, you would not be here. And that's true for everyone else on the planet. All you have to do is go back 30 generations. So, is your life here on Earth at this point in time just an accident or a coincidence? Is it a total statistical improbability? If it is, that's amazing! And if it's not, then that's amazing! It's amazing either way! Your existence should throw you into a state of sheer ecstasy. As Rabindranath Tagore, the famous Indian poet and Nobel laureate, once said, 'If you're not perpetually surprised by the fact of your existence, then you don't deserve to exist.'"

Peter

"That is amazing—it's a straight-forward calculation with an incredible perspective. Who would have guessed?"

Old Man

"Let's go back to our original discussion. Tell me, what do you do on your thinking path?"

Peter

"I think about questions about my life and life in general, sometimes even about the universe."

Old Man

"For example, what kinds of questions?"

Peter

"You know—the tough ones that everybody thinks about at one time or another, like— how did the universe come into existence? Where did I come from? What's the meaning and purpose of life? What's my purpose? What's consciousness and where does it come from? The really tough ones."

Old Man

"I'll say! Have you gotten any answers?"

Peter

In a somewhat dejected tone, he answered, "Honestly—no."

Old Man

"Well, maybe you should try the no thinking approach."

Peter

"Huh? That doesn't make any sense to me." Peter could see the man was a foreigner, but he spoke perfect English with a peculiar, though pleasant, accent. "I've never seen you around Nebušice before. Where are you from?"

Old Man

"I'm from Mesopotamia."

Peter

Peter was puzzled by his answer, but then smiled. "Yeah, right. Mesopotamia, are you kidding me? It no longer exists."

Old Man

"Sure, it does. It's a big part of what you call Syria, Iraq and Turkey."

Peter

Trying not to be too sarcastic, Peter said, "Well, that's quite a distance to travel every day. How in the world do you do that?"

Old Man

"I have my ways."

Peter

Chuckling with disbelief, but then changing to a serious demeanor, Peter said, "Iraq and Syria—terrible places. They've been overrun by war and all kinds of horrible things."

Old Man

"Today, yes, and it's unfortunate, as they were the cradle of civilization. It's in Mesopotamia where I learned how to answer the questions you ask of yourself. But I did it by not thinking, just by being."

Peter

"You must be kidding me."

Old Man

"No, I'm not."

Peter

"Can you share any of those answers with me?"

Old Man

"Eventually, maybe, but first we should get to know each other."

They were quiet for several beats.

Old Man

"Peter, would you like to learn about the power of being?"

Peter

"Sure. Hey! How did you know my name? I never mentioned it."

Old Man

Humorously, "Oh, a lucky guess, I suppose."

Peter

"Yeah, right. And your name is?"

Old Man

"My name in Sanskrit is *Svatantra*. In Czech it would translate as Svoboda, which as you know, in English means "freedom." But, please call me *Boda*."

Peter

"Right. Now what is it you want me to do?"

Boda

"Did you take any challenging courses last semester at ISP?"

Peter

"Sure. Wait a minute, how did you know I attend ISP?"

Boda

"That's easy. It's the only school in Nebušice that could possibly teach you such excellent English."

Peter

"Right, I guess. Yeah, I had a challenging math class—AP Math-501 in advanced calculus and linear algebra.

Boda

"That's pretty hefty for a high school student. Do you think you could find a problem in your textbook that is so difficult, you are unable to solve it?"

Peter

"Sure. That would be easy."

Boda

"Okay. Tonight, I want you to try one of those problems and be sure you cannot easily get the answer. Then, I want you to sit in a quiet place, close your eyes and relax your hands in your lap as you focus on your breath. Take ten slow deep breaths before returning to a natural pace of breathing. For those deep breaths, it's best if you hold your breath for five seconds after inhalation and before exhaling. With each inhalation, mentally say the word '*So*' and with each deep exhalation, mentally says the word *Hum*."

"These words are a mantra and you will be doing a brief meditation, called the *So Hum* Meditation. Try to push all thoughts from your mind, and every time one returns, don't be disturbed by it, simply mentally repeat the mantra, *So, Hum*. After about 30 minutes or so, you can relax, and when you are ready, open your eyes. Then I would like you to again try to solve that same problem and see what happens. Got it?"

Peter

"I guess. But I can't imagine that this meditation thing will make much of a difference."

Boda

"Maybe not. We'll see. Can you be back here tomorrow morning at about 8:00 a.m.?"

Peter

"Sure, then can we talk about the answers to those challenging questions I mentioned to you?"

Boda

"Peter—everything in the fullness of time. See you tomorrow."

Peter
"Yeah, right, okay."

And with that, Peter continued on his way, a bit confused as to what had just happened, but certainly intrigued.

Dialogue 2
Your Path Is The Way

"The right to choose your own path is a sacred privilege."
—Oprah Winfrey

After dinner that evening, Peter went to his room and opened his advanced calculus book, the math course he had just completed during the second semester of his junior year at ISP. He had earned an A. The problems at the end of each chapter were conveniently divided into three categories—green, blue and black. Green problems were not exactly easy, but certainly solvable by capable diligent students taking the course. Blue were difficult. Every now and then Peter was able to solve a one of them. Black were a completely different story. They were very difficult—the students would say, impossible.

They were never assigned by his teacher for any of the homework or exams. Peter had heard a rumor that the black problems were taken from texts used by college upper-class and graduate math majors. No one in his class had ever solved one. He often wondered if even his teacher could solve them.

Peter turned to the black problems at the end of chapter 11, entitled *Vector Analysis*, and arbitrarily chose the third one. He tried to solve it for about thirty minutes when it became apparent to him that he had absolutely no ideas for a strategy to get to the answer provided in the answers section at the end of the book—even when he tried to work backwards from the answer.

He dimmed the light in his room and sat lotus style on the floor next to his bed and began to follow the instructions for meditation provided by Boda. Minutes later, he was in another world, the world of spirit, flooded with endorphins and feeling effects not unlike a runner's high. After 30 minutes, he slowly emerged from his meditation. Peter felt rested, calm and very much at peace—sensations he hadn't recalled feeling for a long time. He thought, *I should be doing this meditation thing every day.* But then awareness took over—*Okay, now for that math problem.*

He reread problem number three and focused on the specific question it asked. Suddenly it seemed to him that one of the theorems he had read in the text might be applicable to solving this problem. He rapidly paged back to it, studied the theorem, and in a flash had an idea on how to use it to set up a calculation strategy that might head in the right direction. He followed through and in less than ten minutes he had an answer. He turned to the answers section in the back of the book. His result was perfectly correct. *How in the world?*

That evening, Peter could barely sleep. He couldn't wait to meet with Boda in the morning to tell him what had happened. Not only did he solve problem number three, but he chose to try problem number five in the black section to be sure what had happened wasn't just a fluke. The same result—could not solve it, but in less than ten minutes after a second crack at meditation, he had the correct answer. This was too good to be true. It was amazing!

In the morning Peter left for the forest at 7:30 a.m. to meet with Boda at 8:00 a.m. It was pouring rain. Even with his hoodie rain parka, he was getting soaked. He sloshed up the mountain as quickly as he could, his boots slipping precariously in the mud as he negotiated the mini-rivulets rushing circuitously down the path. He nearly fell several times, but he managed to keep his balance. He was determined to make his way to the top.

Finally, he was there but Boda was not. Because of the rain, he was probably staying dry in one of the hunting blinds, but which one? There were two to the right on top of the hill and one to the left. He decided on the left. It was closer.

When he got to the blind he called out from below.

Peter

"Boda, are you up there?" No answer. He turned and was just about to leave for the other two blinds when he heard a voice coming from the hunting blind next to him.

Boda

"Yes, I'm here. I was napping. Glad you woke me up. Come on up the ladder and out of the rain."

Peter rapidly climbed up the blind and jumped in under the roof for shelter from the downpour. He breathed a deep sigh of relief to be out of the heavy rain.

Boda

"My goodness Peter, you're soaked."

Peter

"Yeah, it was quite a wet trek getting up here. But, do I have some interesting news for you."

Boda

"Really? Well that's wonderful. But first, please relax for a few minutes. I have a thermos of masala tea and two cups. Let me pour you some so you can warm up a bit."

Boda poured a full cup of tea for both Peter and him. Peter drank his quickly, perhaps to warm his inside, but more probably because he was anxious to finish and tell Boda what had happened the evening before.

Boda

"So, Peter, tell me why all the excitement?"

Peter

"Well, I did exactly what you asked me to do last evening with the difficult math problem and I solved it in no time at all. In fact, I did it twice—two impossible problems—solved in less than ten minutes for each one. It was amazing."

Boda

"I realize you think it was amazing, but it certainly is not to me."

Peter

"I don't understand. These were two incredibly difficult problems. I could never have solved them at my level of training, even though I'm pretty darn good in math. Could that meditation thing make that much of a difference?"

Boda

"Finish your tea, Peter, and then we'll talk about what happened."

Peter

Peter gulped down the rest of his steaming tea. He couldn't wait to hear what Boda had to say. "So again, I just gotta know, could meditation make that much of a difference in my ability to solve a difficult math problem?"

Boda

"Actually, it made all of the difference. As you say, you have excellent skills in mathematics. Otherwise, you wouldn't be taking such an advanced course in high school. But, in order to solve very challenging problems, even clever people need a glimpse of creative insight, something that connects pieces of what they already know, in a way that is not obvious. As biochemist and Nobel laureate, Albert Szent-Gyorgyi once said, 'Discovery is looking at the same thing as everyone else but thinking something different.' Albert Einstein was a genius at this. His thought experiments often provided the insight he needed to choose a path that would lead to the correct answer to the problem he was trying to solve."

Peter

"Is that how he developed the theory of relativity?"

Boda

"In part, yes. Since he's one of your heroes, you may have read that in his research, he imagined what a ray of light would look like if he was on a train moving at close to the speed of light and in the same direction that the ray was moving. The real question is, 'Where did his idea to think like this come from?'"

Peter

"Where did it come from?"

Boda

"Einstein was a very contemplative, let's even say, meditative man. It was his contemplations and meditations that enabled him to connect his astute capabilities in physics and mathematics with a strategy or path to get to the correct answer and develop a theory that would hold up under scientific scrutiny—just like you did last evening. You connected your sharp capabilities in mathematics with the right path—a mathematician would call it a strategy—to get the correct answer to those two difficult math problems. Said another way, to get the right answer to a challenging problem, it's important to ask the right questions."

Peter

"I don't get it. Why should meditation do something as powerful as that?"

Boda

"Ah—now that's the right question."

The rain had stopped, and the sun had started to cast its rays from behind the clouds. Boda and Peter decided to stretch their legs and walk along the ridge for a while. Because they were at the high point of the mountain, it was drier and less muddy than the descending paths. Peter removed his rain parka so that his shirt and jeans could dry. Boda carried his small red carpet under his arm. To avoid splashing mud on the bottom of his tunic, he hiked it up about twenty centimeters and fixed it there by tightening his rope belt.

Although Peter kept pushing for an answer to his question on how meditation could help solve difficult math problems, Boda was not immediately forthcoming. He wanted to think how to provide the answer—which surely would be difficult for Peter to accept—in a way that would be easiest for him to comprehend. They walked across the ridge, gazing periodically into the verdant valley below. Kicking sticks and stones from the path, Boda could see Peter was noticeably impatient with him.

Boda

"Okay, Peter, I'll answer your question. What I am going to tell you is true, tested and reliably correct. It's been known for eons, but because of its ancient history and seeming simplicity, most people have regarded it as a fable or a myth. However, there are some who have put what I will tell you into practice and it has made all the difference in their lives.

Peter

Pushing away any pessimism and trying to be optimistic. he said, "Great! I'm all ears."

Boda

"We need to go back in time, more than three thousand years, to the Indian continent. At that time there were a handful of wise men, spiritualists, you might say, who had lots of time on their hands because they weren't distracted by the chaos and noise that you face in your day-to-day modern world. They were interested in answers to many of those big questions that concern you. Some of them spent long periods of time in meditation just *being* with those questions. This significantly raised their level of consciousness. Something happened when they got to a certain level."

Peter

"Like what?"

Boda

"They began to get creative insights as you did last evening. They found that the longer and deeper they meditated, the more they could extract answers and novel concepts or ideas that normally would never have occurred to them."

Peter

"I can relate to that. For both problems I solved last evening, immediately after meditation I had a thought about a mathematical theorem I hadn't ever considered before and probably would not have done so without meditation. In both cases, that was the magic bullet that led to the solution."

Boda

"It wasn't magic, Peter. That, I can assure you."

Peter

"So then, what was it?"

Boda

"To go back to those wisdom seekers. They found that all people come into this world with a conscious awareness which they called Personal Consciousness. And for reasons they didn't understand at the time, accessibility or connectivity to Personal Consciousness varies from person to person. For those few seekers with high accessibility, even a modest level of meditation enabled them to readily and successfully address or solve difficult problems. For those with less accessibility, it required more time and deeper meditation."

Peter

Peter was dismayed and wasn't sure he was buying Boda's explanation. "This was three thousand years ago—really?"

Boda

"Yes, really. Here's how. Several of these seekers including Rishi Vyas, Patanjali, Varahamihira, Acharya Kanad and Buddha, who had very high levels of consciousness, made a profound discovery. They determined by experiments with meditation that there exists in another dimension, a non-material plane which contains a record of every thought, word, deed or event that has ever occurred or will occur in the future. By accessing information in this plane, they could predict future events with near-perfect accuracy."

"They called this non-material plane the *Akashic Record*. Today, some philosophers and scientists refer to it as the *Akashic Field*.[2] Akasha is a Sanskrit word which means the fifth element—namely, one beyond the four primary elements of alchemy—air, fire, water, and earth. Loosely speaking, the Akashic Record can be considered Cosmic Consciousness, or as some might say, including Einstein, the 'mind of God'. I'll come back to Cosmic Consciousness in another discussion."

Peter

"That's crazy. Is it true? Do you believe it?"

Boda

"Yes, it's true and yes, I not only believe it, I know it. In fact, whether you believe it or not, that's what enabled you to solve those two math problems. You tuned into the *Akashic Record*. It contains an infinite level of knowledge and wisdom and if you are able to connect to it, even to a modest degree, you have the ability to deal intelligently and successful with very difficult issues."

Peter

"If that's correct, I think I'm going to start a daily meditation practice. Next year, I have my Scholastic Aptitude Test, a requirement for college entry, and I must write essays for all my college prospects, especially Harvard. What you're telling me might be just what I need to get into Harvard, my number one choice."

Boda

"I know, for a fact, it would help. But believe me, as we will discuss at another time, it can do more than that, much more. However, for now, I can tell you this. To tap deeper into the Akashic Record for access to greater knowledge and wisdom requires deeper levels of meditation. You're obviously good at the process. For a beginner, you can achieve quite high levels of consciousness through your meditation practice. And therefore, you can enter and access knowledge from the Akashic Record. But to go deeper into meditation and higher in consciousness, you will have to practice."

Peter

"What can I do? I want to get better at this. I can see how it can have great value in my life."

Boda

"In your practice, you first must have an earnest *intention* in your meditation. The ancient wisdom seekers said to do this you should clear your mind of all thoughts for eleven seconds. Don't ask about the number eleven; that's another story and not necessary for now. Next you must put your *attention* on a specific point, for example, a mantra. This you must do for eleven times eleven or 121 seconds, about two minutes. This will increase your level of *awareness* or *mindfulness.* Then comes the hard part—you must focus on a single point with no thoughts for eleven times eleven times eleven seconds, or about twenty-two minutes. At that point you are truly in deep mediation and your consciousness will move to a state where there is no space or time. It will have entered the realm of the great *nothingness,* where nothing exists but infinite possibilities and potential. From here you can choose what you wish to bring into your life."

Peter

"Wow—that sounds incredibly complicated and difficult but seeing what I was able to do with a couple of difficult math problems, I'm willing to give it a try and work at it."

Peter was impatient and wanted to know more. "What about the consciousness aspect of what you mentioned? Can you tell me more?"

Boda

"Yes, but that's also for another day"

Peter

"How about tomorrow? We can go for a hike."

Boda

"Tomorrow is fine, but no hiking for me. It's too much doing and not enough being. Let's meet at 8:00 a.m. at my usual spot, you know, where nobody goes. It's supposed to be sunny tomorrow. I'll bring you a nice carpet to sit on."

Peter

"Great. See you then."

With that Peter headed across the mountain to finish his hike and returned home. He had lots to think about.

Dialogue 3
Consciousness Connections

*"No problem can be solved from the same
level of consciousness that caused it."*
—Albert Einstein

A s agreed, the next day Peter climbed the hill in the
forest and met Boda at the usual place at the end of
the overgrown path and under the evergreen tree near the
crest of the hill.

It was a beautiful summer day, the sun slowly rising and
radiating majestically from the east. Its bright rays made
everything sparkle. Peter felt its energy and looked forward
to his discussion with Boda.

Peter arrived at the top of the hill and approached Boda,
whose eyes were closed while he hummed very strange
sounds. He sensed Peter's presence and greeted him.

Boda

"Namaste, Peter. Come on over. I just finished."

Peter

"Sorry, Boda, I didn't mean to interrupt your prayers or whatever it was you were doing."

Boda

Boda opened his eyes and looked up at Peter. "Oh, just a bit of sound therapy to get me in the mood for our discussion this morning. It brings me greater focus so that I can touch the Akashic Record deeper than usual. That enables my elderly mind to recall the details of important events, especially those which happened billions of years ago."

Peter

"Billions of years? You're kidding, right?"

Boda

"No, I'm not. You'll see in a minute or so. Please sit on the blue carpet there in front of me and make yourself comfortable. I thought you would like blue. It's a very noble color, don't you think?"

Peter

Distant, distracted and seemingly uninterested in the color of the carpet, "Ah, thanks—yeah, I guess so." He sat on the carpet cross-legged and stared at Boda, who was smiling at him.

Boda

"Look, my friend, what I'm about to tell you may sound like religion, but it's far from that. It's spiritual in the sense that it has everything to do with non-material things, but little to do with the three-dimensional world you perceive with your five senses. And it has nothing at all to do with theology."

Peter

Smiling, "That's good. The last thing I need is a good old-fashioned Sunday school lesson."

Boda

Boda smiled as well and continued. "I'm going to share with you concepts from an emerging science known as spiritual physics. It seeks to uncover answers to important questions posed over the ages by scientists and philosophers, questions such as those you shared with me when we first met. Where did I and the universe come from? What's my purpose? Why am I here? What's the meaning and purpose of life—of the universe, as well? Where do I go, if anywhere, after my body dies?"

"These questions might be considered aspects of what modern physicists call the Theory of Everything, or TOE. As you will eventually see, all of this is related in some way to what you experienced after your math-and-meditation experiment. Does that make any sense to you?"

Peter

"I'm not sure, but let's give it a shot."

Because of his interest in physics, Peter had read Brian Greene's popular book, *The Elegant Universe*, in which he talked about the TOE. Peter had a challenge understanding Greene's book to the depth he would have liked to, but he was willing to see where Boda's thoughts would lead. He sat back slightly, supported by his arms outstretched behind him on the soft weave of the blue carpet.

Boda

"These questions are not only big questions; they are *the* questions. But you're an intelligent and gifted young man and if you practice a more comprehensive version of meditation that I will teach you, you can begin to tap deeper into the Akashic Record and understand the answers to these questions. I guarantee it."

Peter

"If I hadn't experienced what I was able to do with those math problems, I'm not sure I'd believe it possible. I'm willing to try."

Boda

"Okay then, let's start at the beginning, although as you'll quickly see, there was no beginning and there will be no end."

Boda could see from Peter's perplexed expression that his comment wasn't making Peter feel any more comfortable. He continued anyway.

Boda

"Our physical universe as we experience it through our five senses reflects something much greater than the universe itself, something well beyond our three-dimensional world. Spiritual physicists call it by several names, the Universal or Infinite Mind, the Unified Field, or as many Buddhists do, Cosmic Consciousness. The name is irrelevant. But what is relevant is that it's a field of energy, a different kind of energy, not treatable by the laws of classical or quantum physics. It is infinite and eternal. It always was and always will be. It occupies every point of the physical universe and extends beyond that into what can be called infinite nothingness, a place, which really is not a place, where nothing exists but Cosmic Consciousness. Einstein would say, 'No space, no time, no energy, no matter—absolutely nothing.'"

Peter

"Well, that's a mouthful—infinite nothingness which is a place that's not a place." Then he thought, *I haven't the foggiest idea as to what he's talking about.*

Boda knew what Peter was thinking. But he wasn't deterred.

Boda

"However, in the words of a quantum physicist, we can say in this non-place there exist infinite possibilities, and under the right circumstances any one of them can be coaxed to pop into our three-dimensional, five-sense world. The fundamental question to which you will soon learn the answer is how do you nudge a desired possibility into your life?"

Peter

This is so weird—a place that's not a place yet it contains a humongous number of possibilities—and I can just grab the one I want and change my life—really?

Peter wasn't buying this yet, but Boda kept on going anyway. He was on a roll and knew that Peter was clever enough and would eventually catch on.

Boda

"All things—absolutely everything—come from this non-place, and eventually return to it in the form of consciousness. Those with a religious orientation might prefer to call it God, but it's certainly not God in the sense taught by any known religion. I remind you of Einstein's favorite quote, 'I want to know the Mind of God. All the rest are details.'[3] As you will eventually see, he was a very perceptive individual—the Akashic Record *is* the Mind of God. And yes, all the rest are simply details."

Peter

"Is there any difference between spiritual energy and the energy of classical and quantum physics?

Boda

"Absolutely. I'll tell you the most significant difference, which is something we will encounter when we speak about the spiritual interactions and communications among people—in fact among all physical and non-physical entities, since all have some level of consciousness."

Peter

"And what's that?"

Boda

"Unlike classical and quantum physics where, according to the theory of relativity, the maximum speed possible for anything, including all known forms of energy, is the speed of light, the speed of spiritual energy moves not only faster than the speed of light, but in fact, it moves instantaneously. Physicists would call it superluminal.

Peter

Peter was trying to stop from twiddling his thumbs and doing his best to be patient, hoping that Boda's explanation would eventually gel into a picture that made sense to him. He decided to change the topic, not realizing he wasn't changing the topic at all. "You mentioned this new science, spiritual physics. What does it say about our purpose and the purpose of the universe, and are they in any way related to consciousness?"

Boda was pleased. Peter asked the right question at the right time. His eyes lit up as he enthusiastically continued.

Boda

"As you might say, you hit the nail right on the head. I told you, you're a smart young man. The purpose of all physical things in our universe, including you, is to enable Cosmic Consciousness—God, if you like—to be continuously, totally and intimately aware of Its own presence. I say 'Its' even though Cosmic Consciousness or God is more genderless than an electromagnetic field—not he, she, or it—spiritual physicists would say it's an energy field, but, as I've said before, not energy in the classical or quantum physics sense, but a spiritual energy. In fact, Peter, we can define consciousness as a spiritual energy field of knowledge and wisdom. It is the true reality or essence of all things, physical and non-physical. In the physical plane, it is most developed in human beings and in the spiritual plane it is infinitely developed in Cosmic Consciousness."

Peter

"So, do spiritual physicists have a clear mathematical and physical sense of how this spiritual energy works?

Boda

"Good question. There's still a lot for them to do to understand the nature of this kind of energy, how it works, how best to access it, and how to use it. But great progress is being made by capable scientists who understand this is our future. The important point for you to comprehend is that your role—the role of everyone and everything in the universe—is to make God intimately aware of Himself. Please excuse the gender, just making the point using the commonly used English pronoun. It works just as well with She, It, or whatever label you want to create."

Boda elaborated. "There are two points I would like to emphasize Buddhists like to say, 'I'was a hidden treasure and wanted to be known.' God wants you to be totally aware of his existence. There is also another aspect exemplified by the famous maxim of the Greek Delphi Oracle, 'Know thyself.' You see, Peter, that's how important you are in the grand scheme of things. God not only wants you to be aware of Him, but just as our five senses provide our awareness of the three-dimensional physical world, the consciousness of all beings and in fact of all material things, living or not, is the means for God to be self-aware."

Peter

Peter couldn't restrain himself. "Hold on. Wait a minute. I'm not a religious person, but even I know that most religions state that God is an all-knowing supreme being. Why in the world would *He* need help from me or anyone or anything else for that matter to know He exists?"

Boda

"As I said before, I am not speaking about conventional organized religions. Cosmic Consciousness—God—is all-knowing, and you could say, supreme. And yes, He knows He exists. He doesn't need you and the rest of the material universe to know that, or about the existence and intricacies of the universe. He's got that down pat. He needs you for *awareness*, just like you need your five senses for awareness of the three-dimensional world. You need your eyes to appreciate the magnificence and beauty of the mountains and the sea, or a Caravaggio painting or a rainbow. Your genius and power are in your mind and most especially in your Personal Consciousness. Your five senses bring awareness to your genius. Without your sight, you would be no less of a genius and without the universe, God would be no less all-knowing or supreme."

Peter

"Your comments about the mutual needs and connection between God and everything in the universe, including me, is amazing. It will take some time for that to sink into my understanding."

"But I have another question about consciousness. What happens when two people connect their awareness, like when my mom is going to say something to me and it's like I can read her mind before she says it."

Boda

"Excellent. That brings me to Collective Consciousness—not to be confused with what psychiatrist Carl Jung called the Collective Unconscious, which refers to the cultural and societal hypnosis or influence we experience by others from birth. That's a subject for another day. Collective Consciousness is consciousness associated with the overlap of consciousness among all species. In fact, every single piece of material matter in the universe, right down to the atoms and subatomic particles that form matter has some level of consciousness. The level of consciousness is miniscule in the smallest of particles, but not zero. And, of course, it's most highly developed in the human species."

Peter

"All species? —are you saying that animals, plants, and non-human organisms have some level of awareness or consciousness? And if that's true and you say that atoms do as well, does that mean every cell in my body is conscious?"

Boda

"That's a question that has been argued for hundreds of years by numerous philosophers and scientists. My answer to both of your questions is an unqualified yes. You see, most modern-day scientists were confounded because they believed that there could not possibly be any consciousness in a human cell. Then some of them did an interesting thought experiment. They reasoned that suppose one were to stack together into the correct structure, somewhere between thirty-three trillion and one hundred trillion cells, and *voila*—you should have a conscious human being. Then those same scientists asked, 'How can that be? How can you stack together trillions of atoms, which they believed had no consciousness, and thereby create a conscious human being? Does that mean, in principle, one could create consciousness?'"

Boda took a deep breath, looked out over the valley, and said to Peter, "Let me tell you about some interesting research done over three decades, beginning in the 1960s. It may put some light on this issue."

"Cleve Backster, a U.S. naval officer during World War II, was a polygraph interrogation specialist. He founded the Central Intelligence Agency's polygraph unit shortly after the end of World War II. After his discharge from the navy, Backster founded a reputable school in New York City, which taught lie detection methodology to the FBI and other law enforcement agencies. He ultimately moved the school, The Backster School of Lie Detection, to San Diego, California, where to date, it has been the longest operating polygraph school in the world."

Peter

"I don't get it. What does lie detection have to do with consciousness or awareness?"

Boda

"Patience, Peter, I'm coming to that. In February1966, Backster's secretary bought him a Dracaena cane plant to dress up his starkly decorated office in New York City. Early one morning, after working throughout the night on some polygraph experiments, he decided to see if his instrument could detect the instant that water fed to the roots of the plant reached its leaves. He reasoned that there may be a signal since the polygraph device functions by measuring galvanic or electric skin response, a phenomenon affected by water content. Individuals not telling the truth emit more moisture through their skin than those telling the truth. The technology is more complicated than that, but that's the general idea."

Peter

Peter jumped into one of his precocious moods. "I still don't get it. What's lie detection got to do with consciousness, anyway?"

Boda

"Patience, my dear boy, I'm coming to that. You see, Backster had been intrigued by research he had read that was carried out in 1900 by a highly recognized Indian polymath and physicist named Jagadish Chandra Bose. Bose found that plants responded to certain kinds of music and grew faster. Backster's reported research findings were amazing. He found that the plant in his office did respond, and in fact gave a signal similar to that observed in humans. He was intrigued, and this set him on an entire new tack for exploring the use of polygraph technology. His findings were increasingly profound—actually unbelievable to many."

Boda was so excited, he was almost beside himself. "Now here comes the role of consciousness. Even more baffling, on the morning of February 2, 1966, during his very first experiment with his Dracaena cane plant, as he sat at his desk after watering the plant and was waiting for a response from the electrodes that were attached to a leaf, he thought, 'This is taking too long. I wonder what would happen if I put a flame under a leaf on this plant?' But before he could get up from his chair to try it, the signal from the polygraph instrument zipped up and off the recorder chart. This result was reproducible. Perplexed, Backster thought. 'This is incomprehensible. Can the plant actually read my mind and in turn respond violently in fear of my vicious intention?' You see, he knew the signal wasn't from the water reaching the plant's roots because he did the experiment again without the water and got the same intense response from the Dracaena cane plant."

Peter

"I don't believe it!"

Boda

"You're not alone. Most scientists didn't believe it either. But Backster wasn't discouraged. These initial experiments and many others subsequently motivated him to begin a detailed research program over a period of thirty-six years concerning the concept of consciousness and awareness in plants and other living organisms. He found that all forms of living organisms can respond to one another, including plants, animal cells, bacteria and live foods such as yogurt. He carried out extensive research with leukocytes, the white blood cells of the human immune system, and found them to communicate with each other. Backster published the results of his research in a book released in 2003.[c]

Peter

"Is Backster's work now being recognized as correct?"

Boda

"Although early on, his work was dismissed by many scientists, recent efforts have found substance in his findings. One article had this to say: 'In the past decade, researchers

---

[c] Clever Backster, *Primary Perception: Biocommunication With Plants, Living Foods and Human Cells*, White Rose Millennium Press, 1st edition, September 2003.

have been making the case for taking plants more seriously. They are finding that plants have a sophisticated awareness of their environment and of each other and can communicate what they sense. There is also evidence that plants have memory, can integrate massive amounts of information and maybe pay attention. Some botanists argue that they are intelligent beings, with a 'neurobiology' all their own. There is even tentative talk of plant consciousness.'"[4]

"More recently, work by Professor Monica Gagliano convinced her that plants studied in her research showed memories and an awareness that most of us would attribute to consciousness."[5]

Peter

Peter didn't know if he was amazed, baffled, or in doubt of Backster's claims. He asked, "Someone must have followed up on Backster's work to see if there was any sense to it, or if it was junk science, right?"

Boda

"Yes, they have, and if you have doubts about non-human consciousness, such as that which is said to exist in plants and their ability to communicate with humans, animals, and with other plants, and would like to read a more scientifically sound analysis, you should consult *Brilliant Green: The Surprising History and Science of Plant Intelligence,* by leading plant physiologist researcher Stefano Mancuso and science writer Alessandra Viola.[6] You can see similar findings in a book entitled, *Plant Sensing and Communication* by Richard Karban, Professor of Entomology at the University of California, Davis."[7]

"You know, Peter, although we may have evolved to a higher level of consciousness than non-humans, there are indications—perhaps caused by the driving hunger of our egos for recognition—that unlike plants and animals, we have lost our way in our Collective Consciousness and its intimate connection to nature. At one time, all human beings could commune intimately with nature. But we have subjected ourselves to the chaos and noise of interfering forces driven by our intense technological hunger for wealth and power."

Peter

"I guess that's why I don't watch the news anymore— Syria, Iraq, Iran, Pakistan, Afghanistan, even the crazy things happening in the U.S. How could our minds be quiet enough to make the nature connection?"

Boda

"You're absolutely right. Eckhart Tolle makes the point that 'Nature exists in a state of unconscious *Oneness* with the *Whole*.'[8] As I said, eons ago we did the same. This, for example, is why virtually no wild animals were killed in the 2004 tsunami disaster in the Indian Ocean, while more than 240,000 people lost their lives. Being more in touch with nature than humans, they could sense the tsunami's approach long before it could be seen or heard. They had time to withdraw to higher terrain. This Collective Consciousness is present in all species, and to the greatest extent in human beings. All we need to do is to wake up, lower the noise level of chaos in our lives, and listen carefully."

They both stopped and looked out over the valley below. Peter couldn't help but comment.

Peter

"You know, this is why I love this mountain and the forest. I walk here every chance I get. I think about these big questions and almost never get an answer that feels right. But you know what? I love the process. I love getting inspired by what I see out here, by what I feel. And, every once in a while, I get an inspiring thought that I love. Isn't that weird?"

Boda

"Not really. You're learning to lower the chaotic noise in the world around you, and when you do, you're touching the Akashic Record and information begins to flow your way. And here is a most important point—if you continue to ask those questions and maintain a regular practice of meditation and just being, you will eventually move into the answers. This I promise."

Peter

"Well, that's good to know, even if it's just a small trickle. Maybe this mumbo jumbo is beginning to make sense." Peter caught himself. "I'm sorry Boda, I didn't mean any disrespect. I guess I'm still tightly connected to modern physics. Spiritual physics is a new concept to me."

Boda

"No offense taken."

Peter

"Thanks. Well, let me ask you something about the consciousness you've described. You've talked about Personal Consciousness and Collective Consciousness. They're starting to become clearer to me. And I guess Cosmic Consciousness is another term for the Akashic Record or God, if you're a religious person. Does that sound right?"

Boda

"Yes, it does, but there is one aspect we haven't discussed and it's the Consciousness Paradox."

Peter

"What's that?"

Boda

"All three are one, yet they're distinctly different."

Boda's comment jarred Peter. He turned to Boda.

Peter

"I'll say that's a paradox."

Boda

"Did you study chemistry?"

Peter

"Yes, last year."

Boda

"Then, let me offer a physical chemistry metaphor that might help you understand what I'm saying. Consider a container of water, where all the water droplets or molecules represent Cosmic Consciousness. Now, let's stir in a fine white powder, the particles of which represent Personal Consciousness. You now have a pure white liquid. Correct?"

Peter

"I guess so. Seems right to me."

Boda

"Next, we slowly stir in a fine black powder that represents Collective Consciousness. As I'm sure you will agree, as I add the black powder, the white liquid turns grey, and the intensity of the grey color increases as I add more black powder. Now let's look at this grey liquid under a powerful microscope. What will you see?"

Peter

"I don't know. I guess you'll see the black particles, the white particles and the water droplets or molecules, if the microscope is powerful enough."

Boda

"Exactly. The three entities, white and black particles and the water droplets are still separate, yet they are one when you observe the grey liquid."

Peter

"Okay, I think I'm beginning to understand. But isn't consciousness really just our mind?"

Boda

"No. It's true that consciousness operates through the mind, the part of our brain that perceives, thinks, reasons, and evaluates. And just as we live at the level of the body, we also live at the level of the mind. The mind, in fact, is pure potential energy. Physics tells us we can convert potential energy into action, namely kinetic energy. In other words, we can change our physical world simply by changing our thoughts and beliefs. That's why most of the self-help literature maintains that 'You are what you believe.' It's true."

Peter

"Since I was a young kid, if I heard that once from my parents, I've heard it a thousand times."

Boda

"They're absolutely right. Let me explain. Consciousness within your mind is a much greater force and extends beyond the mind. It's your spirit, your Personal Consciousness, and it's infinite and eternal and imbued with pure unlimited potential. Tapping into this potential is what enables us to create what some would call miracles. The world out there may seem to be objective, but in fact, it is subjective, something we create by our own interpretations, by our words, our thoughts, and our beliefs. Sadly, most people are unaware of this incredible creative power within them. If they were, most of the problems in this world would soon go away."

Peter

"If that's true, it is an amazing power. Are you telling me that I create my life by focusing my consciousness with my mind, and if I choose to, I can create the physical world I desire by changing my thoughts and expectations?"

Boda

"That's exactly what I'm saying. Put simply, all you need to do is have a specific *intention*, put your *attention* on it, *detach* from the outcome and let the universe handle the details."

"However, there are two rules you must follow to be successful. First, what you want to bring into your life must not hurt anyone or anything and second, in some way it should make the world a better place—even just a little. Your mind is a kind of control valve between the infinite knowledge of Cosmic Consciousness, which contains the entire Akashic Record, and your Personal Consciousness."

"Based on past programming by others, your mind decides how much information from Cosmic Consciousness comes through to your awareness. This can keep important knowledge and wisdom from you. But the positive side of this is that if your mind didn't provide this kind of control, the immense amount of information in the Akashic Record that you would have access to in your five-sense world would overwhelm your human experience."

Peter

"Can we learn to control the valve and open it up for greater access by our Personal Consciousness to the infinite knowledge that's available on the other side in Cosmic Consciousness and the Akashic Record?"

Boda

"You can, but it requires some work. You must reprogram your ego and subconscious to do away with thoughts, notions and beliefs that do not serve you anymore. And that you can do through meditation."

Peter

"Is that difficult to do?"

Boda

"Absolutely not. But it does require a modest and continuous level of effort, and the benefits, as we will discuss later, can be huge."

Peter

"Great, I'd love to hear what you have to say on that. But, one thing bothers me about your definitions of the three types of consciousness. I've read that our mind creates consciousness and awareness. That doesn't agree with what you've said."

Boda

"You're right. You're raising what philosophers and scientists call the Hard Problem, namely, does the mind create consciousness, or does consciousness create the mind? Spiritual physics maintains that consciousness creates the mind."

Peter

"Apparently, I've had the wrong idea about the mind. I always thought that our mind was the source of our consciousness."

Boda

"Yes, most neuroscientists have thought so for decades, but they were wrong. More and more scientists, especially those skilled in quantum physics, are concluding that consciousness creates the mind and not the converse. In fact, in quantum physics there's a phenomenon called the Observer Effect. It states and has been experimentally proven to be a fact that observation creates our three-dimensional reality. We will discuss this some other time."

Peter

"Now that's unbelievable." They had been walking for some time. Peter's legs were growing a bit tired. He turned to Boda. "What do you say we sit on that bench for a while. Some of your ideas are pretty heavy. I think I can focus better if we sit for a while."

Boda

"Sure, I can use a rest."

They sat quietly for a while and then continued their dialogue.

Peter

"Why are some scientists changing their position on this Hard Problem?"

Boda

"Do you know what a near-death-experience, or NDE, is?"

Peter

"Sure, I've read about a number of these and understand that literally thousands of them have been well-documented—people dying for a period of seconds, minutes, or sometimes even more, and then being revived."

Boda

"That's correct. Medical science has shown that during an NDE, when the heart stops beating, seconds later, the brain and mind shut down completely. There are no measurable brain waves. The body is essentially dead—there's no apparent awareness or consciousness. Yet, the person undergoing the NDE has a vivid and clear experience of floating and observing their 'dead' body as well as people in the room. This would be impossible, if consciousness shut down when the brain and mind shut down."

"There are literally hundreds of thousands of documented accounts of people who have gone through an NDE, were revived, and then accurately described things that they observed while they were dead. Even more telling, there have been NDE cases of people with congenital blindness, having never seen a thing since birth. When they are revived, they describe very accurately things they 'saw' in the room where they had 'died.' They describe colors for the first time although they, of course, could not name them."

Peter

"That's amazing! Then, why do many scientists disregard this information?"

Boda

"Because they have a difficult time understanding and studying NDEs. Their scientific instruments don't work for NDEs. They are unable to measure any conventional physical properties during an NDE. The reason is that the science of NDEs falls in the realm of spiritual physics, and a different approach to analysis is required. The laws that govern this area of physics are different than those that govern classical physics or even quantum physics. But we're getting ahead of the story. We'll come back to spiritual physics another time. I would like to return to your question about your purpose and the purpose of the universe. But before I do that, are you clear that consciousness creates the mind and not the converse."

Peter

"Absolutely clear."

Boda

"Excellent. So, let's go to your question about your purpose and the purpose of the universe."

"An important purpose of all life is the continuous and eternal evolution of all consciousness towards Unity Consciousness, namely a state in which we think and act in a manner that unites us spiritually to all others and to Cosmic Consciousness. This is an infinite and eternal process. It had no beginning and will have no end. The current time domain began 13.8 billion years ago with the Big Bang birth of our current universe—a rapid expansion of a single subatomic-size entity physicists call a singularity. Well beyond our comprehension, this microscopic point contained all the energy and mass of our universe. This energy and mass were responsible for the formation of everything in the universe—galaxies, stars, planets, and all living things, including you, Peter, as well."

Peter

"The formation of material things makes sense to me, but I don't get the evolution of consciousness idea."

Boda

"Okay. Look, I 'm sure you have studied biology and the evolution of species. I can tell you that in addition to physical evolution as described by Darwin—survival of the fittest through natural selection to create more perfectly designed and adapted physical species—consciousness throughout the universe is also evolving towards a level necessary for the effective functioning of physically and spiritually advanced species. This is all connected with what we can call the Meaning and Purpose of Life."

Peter

"Can you explain what you mean by the Meaning and Purpose of life?"

Boda

"For now let's just say it in simple terms—the Meaning of Life is to find that special gift you came in to this world with—everyone has at least one—and the Purpose of Life is to share your gifts with others and make the world a better place. Namely, you should be manifesting into this world things that make it a better place and improve your life. That, my dear friend, increases the level of Unity Consciousness. It's all part of the Big Plan."

Peter took a deep breath and exhaled slowly. He couldn't help but be lost in thought.

DIALOGUE 4
THE GENESIS CATASTROPHE

"The universe exists because we are aware of it."
—Martin Rees

As the summer moved on, Peter hiked up the mountain nearly every day to meet and talk with Boda. They enjoyed each other's company, and Peter was learning about the universe and more importantly about himself and the answers to many of the challenging questions he had posed to himself in the past.

It was a hot, muggy, Monday morning in July as Peter hiked along his usual route. Each time he journeyed up the mountain, he was careful to avoid trampling the undergrowth. At least for now, he didn't want to make this route appealing to other hikers. Peter valued his time alone with Boda and didn't want it interrupted. But eventually, he certainly hoped others would have the benefit of Boda's wisdom if he continued to visit Nebušice.

On this morning, Peter was distracted, but not by his usual big philosophical questions and thoughts. He had seen a newscast on TV the evening before and one of the segments bothered him. He wanted to discuss it with Boda. As he approached Boda sitting quietly on his red carpet, he could sense Peter's distress.

Boda

"Good morning, Peter. Come. Sit on your blue throne. After all that rain and mud, we had last week, I had it cleaned for you. I see you have something heavy on your mind. Would you care to share it?"

Peter

Peter looked pensively at Boda for a moment and then said, "Sure, in fact, I'm anxious to hear what you've got to say about it."

Boda

Peter took quite some time to gather his thoughts—too long for Boda. "Well, Peter?"

Peter

"Okay. Last night I watched the evening news. It's not something I do very often. There was a segment covering the current and projected effects of climate change.

Boda

"And?"

Peter

"From what I saw, climate change is not a thing of the future. It's here and now—and it's going to get worse—faster than most of us think. The newscaster said that some islanders in the Asia Pacific are already looking for higher ground on which to live because their homes are being flooded and destroyed by rising seas due to ice melting in the Arctic, Greenland, and Antarctica.

She said that scientific studies show that by 2100 the Maldives will be gone—totally under water. There were film clips of recent hurricanes in the Caribbean. They apparently are becoming more intense due to increasing energy from warmer seas. You probably are aware of Hurricane Katrina and what happened to New Orleans a few years ago."

"The newscaster said scientists project similar global tragedies for the more than three billion people who live on or close to coastal areas. If the figures I heard last evening are even half right, humanity is in store for the biggest tragedy it's ever faced. What are we thinking by doing nearly nothing to minimize the problem? She said scientists feel it's too late to avoid the results of climate change, but at least we should start now to find ways to minimize nature's climatic onslaught and the means to adapt to the coming changes."

Boda

"Wow! That is a mouthful, and yes, probably an accurate insight on a highly probable future for humanity. Let me think for a moment and then try to provide a helpful perspective for what you've shared with me."

Peter didn't say a word. He assumed Boda was plugging into the Akashic Record. Boda closed his eyes and opened them a long several minutes later.

Boda

"Do you know about the Three Laws of Thermodynamics?"

Peter

"Yeah, we covered them briefly in my chemistry course. They have to do with heat and energy and what's energetically possible. They also predict the impossibility of a perpetual motion machine. Why do you ask?"

Boda

"Because I want to make a couple of points. You may know that these laws were not derived mathematically but were uncovered during the 18th and 19th centuries by brilliant scientists and engineers. They are called laws because they make useful predictions, and like Newton's three laws of classical mechanics, they have never been violated and can be used to calculate all kinds of useful and practical things. And yes, there's never been anything close to a perpetual motion machine. So, there is more than a good chance that they never will be violated. Let's accept them as fact."

Peter

Peter hesitated. "Okay."

Boda

"As you may recall, the first law, known as the Law of Conservation of Energy, says that energy cannot be created or destroyed in an isolated system. If we draw a circle around our universe, we are an isolated system. Everything beyond the line—although there are no things there—is the place of nothingness. That's why we say the total energy and mass in the universe is constant. Remember Einstein's famous $E = mc^2$ tells us mass can be converted to energy and conversely, so they are interchangeable."

"But that's not the law I want to talk about. Neither will I digress on the Third Law, which says that entropy, meaning the disorder in an isolated system, is nearly a constant value as the temperature drops 273 °C below zero. It's called absolute zero because you can't go any lower. That's the place where everything—and I do mean everything—stops. Not even one atom can move or jiggle."

"I want to talk about the Second Law, which says that the entropy (disorder or any kind of mess) in an isolated closed system always increases. The only way entropy or disorder can decrease is if work is done on the system. That's the law that can provide you with an interesting perspective on climate change"

Peter

Looking perplexed, Peter said, "Thanks for the review of thermodynamics, but how does the second law clarify things?"

Boda

"Well, let's see. Let's draw an imaginary line around your bedroom. That's our isolated system. The Second Law says that your room, left on its own and not cleaned or tidied, will eventually become messy and disorderly with time. If you do clean your room, the entropy or disorder of the room will decrease, but this will require work and energy by you from outside this closed system to do this. Stated simply, things always get messier with time unless someone does work to prevent it."

"The second law is not only why cleaned rooms become messy with time, but also why ice cubes melt, and why we get older and not younger. Things happen in one direction and not in the other—this is called the 'arrow of time.' The only way things can go backwards is if we do the work necessary to make that happen."

Peter

"I understand. But that still doesn't tell me a thing about climate change and what's happening to the Earth."

Boda

"Patience. I'm getting there. I just want to be sure we are on the same page. So, now let's draw a line around the outer atmosphere of Earth and call it a closed system. The Second Law tells us that over time entropy or disorder will increase unless something from outside this closed system in the universe reaches inside and does work and expends energy to prevent this disorder from happening—some might call it the hand of God. But I can absolutely assure you that is not going to happen."

Peter

"So, are you telling me that the Earth is continuously bound for increasing disorder for as long as it exists?"

Boda

"Exactly. When there is a closed system such as the Earth containing the presence of active chemistry and biochemistry and no constructive work towards maintaining a fixed order from outside the system, in this case by the universe, the system will always proceed towards maximum disorder. The key question is how quickly this occurs. It could be geologically nearly instantaneously such as the Permian-Triassic extinction event, which happened 250 million years ago due to huge volcanic eruptions that released massive amounts of CO_2 into our atmosphere. The Earth heated up and its oceans nearly came to a boil. In a very short geological timeframe thereafter, 96 percent of all marine life and 70 percent of land species died off. It took millions of years to recover. There have been five such massive extinctions in the Earth's 4.54-billion-year history."

Peter

"God, that's frightening! Have they all been caused by changes on Earth, like a massive volcanic eruption?"

Boda

"Not all, but most. One, which was caused by something from outside of the closed system we have defined by our imaginary line around the Earth, namely from the surrounding universe, was the last one which happened about 66 million years ago. Called the Cretaceous Extinction event and caused by the collision of a massive meteor with the Gulf coast of Mexico, it was ultimately responsible for killing off the dinosaurs. Ironically, their demise eventually enabled the evolution and diversification of small to medium size mammals, including human beings. Those huge over-sized carnivores were dining on every piece of meat they could find."

"But here's an important point. There have been five such massive extinctions in the Earth's history. A few have occurred in the geological blink of an eye, meaning over hundreds of years. There are others that took some time to unfold. One of them actually is responsible for your survival."

Peter

"Really? Like how?"

Boda

"Ironically, it's called a catastrophe—the great Oxygen Catastrophe. It will take a bit of explanation, but I think you'll appreciate the irony of it."

Peter

"Great. Let me hear it."

Boda

"About 2.5 billion years ago, the process of evolution reached the level of cellular life that we know today—membrane-encased, multi-protein structures, under the command of gene-bearing DNA—all made possible by the action of enzyme catalysts. As you may be aware from your chem course, a catalyst is a chemical structure which speeds up chemical reactions—and the best catalysts form only the desired product and no byproducts."

"Mother Earth had breathed her first breath of what would eventually give way to contemporary life. Our very first ancestors, bacteria, were born. We call them prokaryotes—cells without a nucleus—to distinguish them from future, more advanced generations called eukaryotes—cells, mostly with nuclei, which evolved from their prokaryote predecessors."

"What is so incredible is that our bacterial ancestors were the only creatures to occupy the planet for the next 1.5 billion years, when finally, the first eukaryotes appeared as improved and more efficient organisms in the evolutionary process. Mother Nature is very patient."

Peter

"I just love the way you call these cells our ancestors."

Boda

"Well, they are. Think of this. Your body contains trillions of microorganisms, outnumbering human cells by 10 to 1. But, because of their small size, they make up only about three percent of your body's weight. I'm guessing you weigh 150 pounds. That means you carry around nearly five pounds of bacteria."

Peter

"Lovely—I hope they're the friendly kind for digestion and whatever."

Boda

"I'm sure they are. But going back to your ancestors—during their early tenure on Earth, they had plenty of time to develop the rules of the game. They learned to live cooperatively in symbiotic alliances with one another—a good history lesson for us humans. Using enzyme catalysts as their primary tools, they survived and evolved their way through the greatest crisis the Earth has ever endured."

Peter

"This I gotta hear and how they did it?

Boda

"They accomplished this during these early days by learning (evolving) to function quite nicely in the Earth's then vile atmosphere of highly toxic gases, namely, hydrogen sulfide, carbon dioxide, carbon monoxide, methane, and nitrogen—no oxygen. Believe it or not, it would have been a deadly gas to them. Our bacterial ancestors manufactured enzyme catalysts within their cellular structure to help them munch on, digest and assimilate these dreadful toxic molecules as a food source. The catalysts in their cell structure ate these toxic gases and excreted byproducts of hydrogen, carbon, nitrogen, and sulfur, all atoms basic to our current structure of life."

Peter

"Now that's cool. I guess those molecules came in handy eons later when human beings evolved."

Boda

"You're absolutely right. But first there came a huge crisis. Eventually there evolved a roving maverick, a bacterial relative to a modern species called cyanobacteria. You can find them today in the greenish muck that floats on any stagnant pond. These guys tired of eating hydrogen from atmospheric gases like methane and hydrogen sulfide, probably because both gases were decreasing in their availability from the atmosphere."

"And so, what did they do? These purple and green microbes sought out the biggest source of hydrogen food they could find on Earth—water. They evolved their DNA and ancillary catalytic apparatus to be capable of biting into those strong hydrogen-oxygen bonds that hold the architecture of water molecules so tightly together."

"As these new bacteria learned to chew on water, they excreted oxygen gas, which at the time was toxic to all living bacterial species. And 2 billion years ago, these microbial villains started what biologist Lynn Margulis has called the 'oxygen holocaust,' the worst worldwide pollution crisis ever endured by any living species on Earth. Again, in the blink of a geological eye, the concentration of oxygen in our atmosphere jumped from nearly zero to its present level of 21 percent. Many of our bacterial ancestors were wiped out—oxidized, burned to a crisp by a kind of spontaneous combustion. Unlike cyanobacteria, they weren't equipped to function in an oxygen environment."

Peter

"Oh my God, that is so weird, so crazy. What happened after that?"

Boda

"Not to worry. The overall system of our forefathers was not only programmed to survive, but to prosper. In time, some of the surviving cyanobacteria evolved a new catalytic metabolic system, one that required the very toxin they excreted, oxygen. Incredibly, these microbes invented a life-support system which was uniquely tailored to this new world. In one organism, they had designed and built a catalytic apparatus for both photosynthesis, which produced oxygen gas, and respiration which consumed it. It was a magnificent triumph."

"Surviving this cataclysmic event was but one example of the many evolutionary miracles our microbial ancestors worked as they adapted and improved their situation with time. Over the long haul, those prokaryotes developed all the rules and regulations for living with each other in an ever-changing environment. They prepared the way for the coming of their more efficient great grandchildren, the eukaryotes—the kind of cells that make up we human beings."

Peter

"That's an interesting geological history on evolution, but what does that say about climate change? I'm really concerned about all the CO_2 we're pumping into the atmosphere that's not just heating up the planet, but also destroying the oceans. From what I learned on that newscast, one-third of this CO_2 ends up in the oceans almost immediately, and when CO_2 dissolves in water, it apparently forms carbonic acid, which can destroy marine life, reefs, and just about everything in the sea. The newscaster said some scientists are saying that what we are currently doing to the oceans has the potential to make devastating changes that haven't been seen in more than 300 million years."

"If that doesn't scare us, she closed with another frightening fact. Increasing temperatures in our atmosphere and oceans are warming the global permafrost. Apparently, permafrost contains huge amounts of encapsulated methane gas, which when released is 30 times more effective than CO_2 in warming our atmosphere. If that's not enough to concern you, apparently there are trillions of tons of methane trapped at the bottom of the oceans at various places throughout the globe. As the oceans warm these so-called methane clathrates will decompose and bubble violently out of the oceans."

"Like, it's very scary. What can we do?"

Boda

"There are a couple of points here. On Earth, as long as there are biological species, such as humans, and chemically active elements, like minerals, oceans, and volcanoes, the Second Law of Thermodynamics tells us there will always be movement towards disorder, chaos, if you like, even without external interference from outside the system—like meteor impacts. Changes caused by intelligent species like humans, as opposed to those caused by unintelligent species such as cyanobacteria, have only one parameter to be effectively managed, namely, the rate of change or the time period over which these changes take place—especially if effective adaptation strategies are to be implemented."

Peter

"So, I get from what you're saying, it's inevitable—climate change is going to happen just as it has in the past. We have two options as intelligent, knowledgeable human beings. The first is for all of us to give up and join the climate deniers and let what happens happen over the next several decades—seas rise two to three meters and flood much of humanity, mega-storms destroy lots of lives and trillions of dollars of infrastructure beyond repair, all causing the outbreak of civil unrest as much of humanity finds itself fighting for its existence and with little to lose. The second option is to accept the reality of what we have done or not done to facilitate climate change and work diligently to put in place the infrastructure and systems to slow it down and have sufficient time to adapt to what changes will occur."

Boda

"Bravo, Peter! There are no other choices. Climate change is here and is accelerating. The question is, as you precisely perceive, how can we work together to slow it down so that we can adapt to its impact and minimize the damage and calamity to humankind? This will require a much more effective unification of all people, especially corporations and governments—very challenging. Things don't seem to be going anywhere near that direction. Unfortunately, sometimes it takes a minor catastrophic event to unify people of different values—otherwise Earth may face its sixth mass extinction, this time cause by the most highly evolved and intelligent species on the planet. It would be called the great global anthropogenic ecological catastrophe."

Peter left Boda that after noon more informed about realities and options, but no less concerned about humanity than he had been when he'd gone up the mountain that morning.

DIALOGUE 5
CONSCIOUSNESS-BODY
CONNECTION

"Control of consciousness determines the quality of life."
— **Mihaly Csikszentmihalyi**

It was raining heavily Tuesday morning. Peter awoke with a start, much earlier than usual. He lay in bed feeling somewhat depressed after yesterday's meeting with Boda. It wasn't something he experienced very often. He wished it would just be gone.

He thought for a moment—*thermodynamics, closed systems, disorder, chaos—climate change—and no one's doing a damn thing about it. What a wonderful future we've got in store for us.*

He had a hard time getting up and barely ate a thing, which was a first for him. He usually downed a large healthy breakfast before leaving home in the morning. Most astonishingly, he decided to forgo his daily visit with Boda.

He sulked around the house most of the day, trying to read and listen to music. Nothing worked to distract him from his negative thoughts except for a long nap he managed late that afternoon. After dinner he decided to watch TV as a diversion from his troublesome thoughts. This was something he rarely did anymore. After a few hours, he wasn't even sure which programs he had watched.

As late evening approached, Peter finally surrendered to a nearly silent voice in the back of his mind encouraging him to meditate and then go to bed. He felt it had been a terribly useless day. As he sat in the chair in his bedroom, he worked as diligently as he could to quiet his thoughts, as Boda had taught him. Because of his negative disposition, it took him some time to properly focus.

His mind finally went blank. It wasn't but a few minutes when he suddenly began to sense the same thought over and over. It was something Boda had mentioned to him several times: "Not to worry—you're not a physical being having a spiritual experience. You're an infinite, eternal spiritual being having a physical experience. Your five senses and your mind—conscious, subconscious and ego—mask your knowledge of your spiritual nature. Wake up and see your true reality."

Peter made a mental note to remember Boda's advice as he slipped into a deep sleep—just what he needed. He was mentally and emotionally exhausted.

The next morning, Peter awoke abruptly at 6:00 a.m. After his usual hefty breakfast, he left for the forest and followed the rising sun up the path. He had to speak with Boda.

The climb cleared his head a bit and it wasn't long before he and Boda were face to face.

Boda

"Good morning, Peter. My goodness, you again seem to have all the troubles of the world sitting on your shoulders. And you didn't join me yesterday for our usual morning chat. Do you have a problem with Tuesdays? What's going on?"

Peter

"No, no, it's nothing like that. Things are not as bad as when I left you on Monday. I guess I needed a break to think, or maybe to try not to think. Every time I tried to rationalize or understand our discussion on climate change, I felt sick. I guess I resented the fact that we, the younger generation, will not only inherit the disturbing future our immediate ancestors have prepared for us, but as I look around, they are not doing a damn thing to address the problem."

"In some cases, politicians and industrial leaders, who are aware of the problem, don't seem committed to do a damn thing. From what I can see, corporations feel it will cost too much money— 'There goes our stock price.' Politicians don't want to divert funds from special interest groups to climate change— 'There goes my votes in the next election'. It's terrible."

"But last night I did one of those deep meditations you taught me. Afterwards, I fell almost immediately into a deep sleep and woke up this morning feeling better, but certainly still concerned about our future."

Boda

"Why do you think you feel better?"

Peter

"I'm not sure. But something happened during my meditation. I kept hearing your comment about not being a physical being having a spiritual experience, but rather an infinite, eternal, spiritual being having a physical experience. Somehow, it gave me hope for a better future—although, I'm still bothered by thoughts of the effects of climate change on the Earth's future and the fact that governments and corporations don't seem to care enough to do something about it."

Boda

"Don't worry about the Earth. Billions of years of history have taught us that she always bounces back over time. I think you probably mean humanity's future."

Peter

"Yeah, right. I just don't know what we can do about it."

Boda

"Well, even though it may not seem like it, there is a huge presence of consciousness rising to ever higher levels within humanity. Although it may well require a misstep to push this consciousness over the tipping point to physical action on our part, I think there is hope for us."

Peter

Somewhat jokingly, he said, "That's the best news I've heard all day!"

Boda smiled and was pleased to see that Peter was feeling better about their conversation on Monday. He continued.

Boda

"The cosmos or better yet, Cosmic Consciousness wants everything to work out for us. But free will is alive and well, and we often get in the way and slow things down or make problems for ourselves. In any case, the reason you kept 'hearing' that thought during your meditation is because Cosmic Consciousness wants to remind you that your true reality is spiritual—it's consciousness and it's infinite and eternal. So, don't worry. Your body is not your reality and besides, it just comes and goes anyway. The problem is that most of us, because of much indoctrination since birth, are not happy with the goes part."

Peter

"What do you mean by 'it comes and then goes'— obviously more than we are born and eventually die, right?"

Boda

"You're right. It's quite a magical story. Let me share with you some thoughts about your amazing body, which you may not be aware of. You see, you can observe the power and connectivity of consciousness with your body in your everyday physical being and activities. In fact, if this connection did not exist, life as we know it would be impossible. From the moment of conception to the instant of death, it's the spiritual force of consciousness that orchestrates all that you do—everything without exception. That's spiritual physics in action."

"Your body is composed of about 40 trillion cells, a number that is more than 100 times the number of stars in the Milky Way galaxy, celestial home to our solar system and planet Earth. Every one of those cells—the majority of them are bacteria, remnants of our distant relatives— measures less than 1/1000 of an inch (2.5 microns) in diameter and contains instructions within its DNA that would fill 1,000 books, each book being 600 pages long— an amazing 600,000 pages of critical instructions. Every one of those cells performs nearly 100,000 biochemical reactions or activities every second, and each cell instantly harmonizes and correlates its activities with every other cell in your body. You might think, "How in the world does it do that?"

Peter

"Exactly—even after an Advanced Placement course in biology, I have no idea how that could ever be possible, certainly not by conventional chemistry and physics."

Boda

"Well, I'll tell you, it is possible, and it's happening right now in your body as we speak. That group of 40 trillion cells works as a strong cooperative team, supporting each other with absolute precision, harnessing all the resources they have at hand. If not, there could be illness, and in the worst case, possibly death. It would be impossible for a human being to live and function properly if there was not a mechanism for this instantaneous communication and orchestration among the trillions of continuous cellular reactions occurring over the lifetime of your body. This is the miracle of life at work and one of the roles of your Personal Consciousness."

Peter

"That's mindboggling. What causes this orchestration and communication among these trillions of cells?

Boda

"It's based on one of the laws of spiritual physics, known as the Law of Nonlocality. It asserts that energy or matter that was ever in close contact, even when separated by cosmic distances can communicate instantly, faster than the speed of light. And since the source of all energy and mass was in intimate contact in that singularity we talked about, which gave birth to the universe some 13.8 billion years ago, your cells have no problem instantly communicating with each other.

Peter

"I guess you could say this is a practical and critical cooperation between my physical and consciousness systems."

Boda

"Absolutely. But think about this: When do these two systems come together for the first time? Let me try to make things a bit clearer. Observed at the molecular level, more than 99 percent of your body is carefully and uniquely constructed by the forces of nature from only six common atoms—carbon, oxygen, hydrogen, calcium, nitrogen and phosphorus—with a very minute sprinkling of several others minor ones such as sulfur, iron, potassium, sodium and magnesium."

Peter

"Suppose we were to do one of those thought experiments like Einstein used to do when he was creating the Theory of Relativity? Remember when he saw himself on a train going at the speed of light in the same direction of a light beam. In our thought experiment, suppose we were to put all those atoms together in the right way to make a human being. Could we make a conscious person?"

Boda

"If we were to assemble the appropriate combination and distribution of those atoms—I calculate we would require 260 trillion-trillion atoms (26 followed by 25 zeros) drawn from the list I just mentioned—the result would be a 150 pound (68 kilogram) human being.

Peter

"Yeah, but would it be a conscious being like us?"

Boda

"That's an excellent question. The answer is no, not yet. An infinite eternal web of Personal and Cosmic Consciousness exists which can at its 'will' assume operation of this human structure. The ancient wisdom seekers would say that this connection is made at the moment of conception—when the sperm connects to the ovum. It is at that moment that a specific spirit with its Personal Consciousness chooses to be born again and occupy what will eventually grow in the womb of its mother and finally be born as a human being. Those wise seekers, in the spirit of Buddhist philosophy, would also say this is a mechanism for dealing with karma generated during past lives."

"Although some level of consciousness does exist in all physical matter down to the last vestige of subatomic particles, the sum total of this consciousness due to the trillions of atoms in any human being is not sufficient to manage and orchestrate its normal operation. Humankind is the first species since the beginning of life on our planet to have total awareness as a key element of Personal Consciousness. This awareness occurs because of the unification of the body with Personal Consciousness during that first moment of conception. We are the first species capable of asking and struggling over deep questions such as those posed by you—inquiries like, 'Who am I?' 'What is the nature of the universe?' and 'What is my purpose?'"

Peter

"Wow. It seems like consciousness is everything. Why does it even need the body?"

Boda

"Because the overall cosmic objective is to continuously increase the level of consciousness in the universe and unite this consciousness as part of the whole, namely Unity Consciousness. This can only be done by occupying a physical body. The spirit chooses a body to be born into and does its best to increase the level of its Personal Consciousness over the lifetime of the body it occupies before that body dies. The spirit is subsequently born again into a new body, and the process starts over again. It's an eternal process working towards infinite Unity Consciousness."

Peter

"It's nice to know our body has some value in helping the spirit evolve. I was wondering if you say more about Unity Consciousness and why we strive to bring it to hire levels?"

Boda

"Sure. You see, living only in the five-senses physical world, we tend to believe all beings are separate and have limited resources. From this perspective, we often think If someone else finds success, we may be left out. We become steeped in a competition and this pits us against one another and prevents us from experiencing true happiness and fulfillment."

"However, at both the molecular and spiritual levels, we are all truly one sharing the *unity* of our all-pervasive inter-connected spirit—Collective Consciousness. Once we realize we are connected, the notion of competition disappears, giving way to cooperation and Unity Consciousness."

"In the state of Unity Consciousness, we know that when one person succeeds, we all succeed. On the deeper spiritual level, we are not only related to our family, but to the entire world. When we realize this, we live in *unity,* celebrating everyone's success. As we move closer to Unity Consciousness, it becomes increasingly clear that our own Personal Consciousness is connected to all others through Collective Consciousness."

"But now here's an important message. When enough people come to this realization that we are truly one and release the perception of separateness, we can achieve a critical mass of Unity Consciousness that will not only benefit our own lives but will also heal the world. And this, Peter, is what the world needs to address the critical challenges it currently faces."

Peter

"That is an important message. I guess I need to work at increasing my Personal Consciousness."

Boda

"Actually, your Personal Consciousness is not growing in amount. It's true that it achieves higher and higher levels as time travels forwards, but its essence remains the same. It is the body that continuously changes. It's kind of like you on the first rung of a ladder. You're the same 'you' on the first and last rung. The only thing that changed was the height at which you functioned. Let me provide another example. If you meditate deeply, you can access further into the Akashic Record and have the benefit of a broad spectrum of knowledge. Your Personal Consciousness has not changed. It simply moved to a higher level so that greater access to knowledge and wisdom is now available to you."

Peter

"That's clear and it's amazing, but what do you mean by, 'It's the body that changes?'"

Boda

"Your physical body which was here on Monday is not the same physical body you have today. That's because with each breath you inhale about 1×10^{22} (1 followed by 22 zeros) atoms from the universe. With every breath that you exhale, you breathe out 1×10^{22} of these atoms. Most of the atoms in these molecules originate in the cells of your body. At the atomic level you are literally breathing out bits and pieces of your liver, heart, brain tissue and more. Technically speaking, we all are intimately sharing our bits and pieces with each other through every breath we take. As Walt Whitman wrote in his poem *Song of Myself,* 'For every atom belonging to me as good belongs to you.'"

"This is no longer simply a metaphor of poetry. It's a scientific fact of biology. If we draw an imaginary spherical container around the Earth, and recognize the dynamic equilibrium and exchange of atoms and molecules within the atmosphere with all living matter on the planet, we can calculate beyond a shadow of doubt that right at this moment, you have in your body at least one million atoms that were once in the bodies of John Lennon, Prince, Elvis Presley, or anyone else you might care to imagine."

"Because of this constant exchange of atoms and molecules around the globe, in just the last three weeks a quadrillion (1 x 10^{15}—namely, 1 followed by 15 zeros) atoms have gone through your body that have also gone through every other living species on this planet. So, envision a camel in Morocco, a taxi driver in New Delhi, a hawk in Mongolia— you have atoms in your body right at this very moment that were circulating through those bodies only three weeks ago."

Peter

"Who would have thought?"

Boda

"In fact, in less than a year, you replace more than 98 percent of all the atoms in your body by exchanging them with atoms from the global environment. At the atomic level, you recycle your liver every six weeks, your skin once a month, your stomach lining every five days, your skeleton every three months. Even the atoms in your DNA, which hold the memories of millions of years of evolutionary time—the actual raw materials: carbon, oxygen and hydrogen—come and go every six weeks like migratory birds. So, if you think you are your physical body, you have a bit of a dilemma. Which one are you talking about? —the one who was here on Monday, or the one that's sitting in front of me right now?"

Peter

"Even the atoms in our DNA?"

Boda

"Yes, even the atoms in your DNA. However, as consciousness—and by that I mean your memories, dreams, imagination, inspiration, intuition, insight, creativity, and choice-making—you are constantly outliving the 'death' of the atoms and molecules of your living physical body through which you express and tend to define yourself. Then in fact, in 'reality," you must not be your body. As Shakespeare reminded us in the *Tempest,* 'We are such stuff as dreams are made on.'"

Peter

"I get that you're telling me my true reality is my Personal Consciousness, not my body. That's challenging enough to understand and accept, but then you say I'm eternal and infinite—I've got quite ways to go to get that."

Boda

"I know, it's difficult because of the social and cultural hypnosis you, like most people, have endured from the moment of birth. It is this programming that incites within you what the Buddha called the four sources of all suffering:

1. Not knowing your true reality—namely, consciousness, and not your physical body
2. Grasping and clinging fearfully to that which is impermanent

3. Identifying with the socially induced hallucination called the ego
4. Fear of death

"These four fears can actually be distilled down to three—not knowing your true reality; fear of impermanence; and identifying with your ego. Once you get over these fears and recognize that the real you is here forever, you'll completely lose your concerns for physical impermanence."

Peter

"Intellectually, I understand what you're saying, but spiritually, it's going to take some time for me not to worry about the impermanence of my body and all those around me, and for that matter—about climate change. I'm not sure I can do it in this lifetime."

Boda

"Not a problem—there are as many future lifetimes as you need." Boda smiled, "Until tomorrow, Peter."

Peter

"Yeah, right—until tomorrow . . ." From Peter's hesitant response, Boda could see he wasn't quite sure about Boda's solution to the 'problem.'

DIALOGUE 6
THREE BLIND MINDS

*"There is no aspect of reality beyond
the reach of the human mind."*
—Stephen Hawking

As summer edged towards fall, rain or shine, Peter didn't miss a day to meet with Boda. Always thought-provoking, their conversations often left him with a deep sense of awe for the universe and his place in this vast, seemingly eternal expanse. But on occasion he left the mountain more perplexed and unsettled than when he'd arrived that day. No subject was more mystifying than their dialogue concerning the human mind.

It was a sullen overcast day in August as Peter made an early start up the mountain. He had told Boda several days before that he was really getting into ancient wisdom philosophies. He was becoming increasingly impressed by what he was reading in a book entitled, *How to Know God—The Yoga Aphorisms of Patanjali*.[9] Boda had given him a copy as a way to more fully understand the spiritual concepts they had been discussing, and told him the book was based on a philosophy and had nothing to do with any of the principles of organized religion.

Peter

"One of the most interesting and sometimes disconcerting concepts I'm learning about from Patanjali is his ideas about the nature of the mind. His comments often blow me away. They're always amazing, sometimes hard to comprehend, and often difficult to accept."

Boda

"That's understandable, especially since neurologists, philosophers and psychiatrists continue to debate the nature of the mind and whether it exists within or outside the body. For our purposes, as you know from our discussions over the summer, I follow the path of ancient wisdom traditions because it all fits together beautifully, scientifically and metaphysically. In this regard, as we discussed previously, based on lots of near-death experiences, NDE studies, it's quite clear that consciousness creates the mind and not the converse. Therefore, consciousness must exist outside the body."

Peter

"That seems right, I guess—at least from what we've discussed previously and what I've read in Patanjali book. Let's see if I got it right. You said that Personal Consciousness, Collective Consciousness, and Cosmic Consciousness are eternal and infinite. But the mind is mortal and exists in space and time. I guess you could say that space is the brain within our skull. And when you die, goodbye brain and goodbye mind. Right?"

Boda

"Correct. The mind begins to evolve shortly after conception and ceases to exist when the person dies. Whereas all the elements of consciousness that are not generated by the mind, as you've correctly understood, are eternal and infinite. They have always been and always will be."

Peter

"There seems to be two types of consciousness, one generated by the mind and that which is infinite and eternal, namely, Personal, Collective and Cosmic Consciousness. Is there some kind of connection between them?"

Boda

"Some elaboration may help. Because your Personal Consciousness is infinite and eternal, it has complete awareness before your birth, during your life, and subsequent to your death."

Peter

"Yes, but my mind is working and it's aware. Isn't it conscious?"

Boda

"Yes, the mind does have awareness, which is strictly the result of your functioning brain and therefore operates only during your lifetime. This awareness is the result of a healthy mind, which can be divided into three parts— your conscious mind, your subconscious and your ego. Interestingly, your mind is often confused and thinks it's the seat and source of all your consciousness, which of course, isn't true. Sure, it's a form of consciousness, but it's temporary, and functions only while you are alive. Personal Consciousness is your true, eternal and most powerful awareness."

Peter

"What's the difference between consciousness created by the mind and Personal Consciousness?"

Boda

"The functioning of your mind is the result of ever-increasing levels of neural hard-wiring which, like a computer, stores knowledge and memories. That begins to occur immediately upon the mind's formation within the womb. This hard-wiring is primarily experienced-based, with increasing levels of mental content accumulating in your brain's hard-wired storage as you continue to learn things from various sources. Scientists believe your mind and thus physically-based consciousness are primarily associated with what is known as the thalamocortical complex in your brain. Most neurologists maintain that this part of the brain is fully formed and functioning between the 24th and 28th week of gestation.[10] Even though physical consciousness is generated by the mind, it is also eternally recorded in the Akashic Record for future access and use—remember, it records every thought, word and event.

Peter

"I guess I'd better be careful what I think about. Does that mean the brain is completely formed and working at that time? I mean is the fetus beginning to think and reason?"

Boda

"Not completely. About two months after conception, electroencephalographic (EEG) signals across both cerebral hemispheres of the fetus demonstrate that its brain is now in a state of full neural integration, which means all existing mental hardwires are connected. Scientists believe that by the third trimester, all these neurological circuits are functioning for mind-based consciousness. The neural networks that form within the brain and constitute the mind interact continuously with Personal Consciousness, Collective Consciousness and Cosmic Consciousness. But remember that unlike mind-based consciousness, which receives an initial kick-start during the third trimester of pregnancy, these three forms of consciousness have been functioning forever."

Peter

"Honestly, Boda, how can you know all this stuff?"

Boda

"Let's just say, as you might in my place, 'Been there, done that!'"

Peter

Somewhat confused, but not wishing to push Boda further, Peter changed the subject, "Right. Now what about intelligence—how does that fit in this whole picture?"

Boda

"Both your IQ (Intelligence Quotient) and your EQ (Emotional Quotient) depend on three components. The first is due to a small level of knowledge leakage that has moved beyond the reincarnation firewall from past lives.[11] This is often the source of what some call a *déjà vu* experience."

"The second is from knowledge accumulated by your experience with various physical and spiritual sources."

"And the third is due to the level and effective operation of the brain's hard-wired neural networks, namely, how efficiently the mind's hardware in the brain's structure operates. However, all these aspects of intelligence have their source in Personal Consciousness and Cosmic Consciousness. The mind then is simply a mirror that reflects this intelligence."

"And one last point—it is the level of your Personal Consciousness that determines how effective you are in tapping into the knowledge and wisdom of the Akashic Record. From your experience, you now know that the primary tool to raise this level is meditation."

Peter

"I'll say. Solving tough math problems has never been easier for me.

Boda

"Glad to hear that. Now here's an interesting point to consider. You may encounter people with highly developed neural hardwiring. They appear to be geniuses and maybe are straight-A students, however, with only a modest level of consciousness. They may rarely make big leaps of creativity, discovery, and invention. Then, there are those individuals who have a good IQ—perhaps, B-students— but have high levels of consciousness. It is often they who make the great leaps of thought that result in significant discoveries and innovations. Of course, there are those who have both sets of attributes and are very gifted individuals."

Peter

"Are there any examples in history of those creative B-student types that I might know. You know, the ones who went on to make big contributions?"

Boda

"Sure, your hero, Albert Einstein was an excellent example. Some have said he was a B+ student when he was in school. But when developing the theory of relativity, he was surrounded by math geniuses, whom he often consulted—mathematicians such as David Hilbert, Henri Poincare, Hendrik Lorentz and John Von Neumann.

Their input was helpful in guiding Einstein to a strategy that enabled him to see the physics and mathematics he needed to create the theory of relativity. But it was Einstein whose elevated consciousness gave him a picture of how to put all the pieces together for a successful theory. He was an expert at looking at the same thing as others but thinking differently."

Peter

"That's amazing. I sure would like to understand the real nature of the mind, that is, without becoming a neuroscientist."

Boda

"The best source of wisdom on the nature of the mind comes from the spiritual avatar, Patanjali, which is why I gave you his book. He lived sometime between the fourth century B.C.E and the fourth century C.E.[12] Very little is known about him and precisely during which period he lived because much of his teachings were handed down orally, until some centuries later when they were written down by wisdom scribes. The fundamental elements of Patanjali's insights were presented and preserved as oral aphorisms, namely, short pithy statements that contain a concise fundamental truth. For example, *identifying consciousness with that which merely reflects consciousness is egoism*. The aphorisms of Patanjali have been among the most respected and frequently quoted wisdom over the ages."

Peter

"I find it mindboggling to read his book and realize its contents were created thousands of years ago. Much of it seems to agree with modern science. For example, his idea of the cosmology of the universe is nearly exactly what modern scientist are saying now. In fact, the translators state in the book that scientifically-minded students should compare Patanjali's cosmology with the latest concepts of a quantum physics, and they will be surprised at how many points of resemblance exist between the two systems. How can that be?"

Boda

"Because although Patanjali was a person, he was also divine. Today, you would call him an Avatar—a human being with a very high level of consciousness and therefor, total access to the Akashic Record—what some call the mind of God. That's a whole other story, but for now allow me to explain a little further his concept of the mind. I think it may help answer some of your questions"

"As you may have read in the book, Patanjali divides the mind (*chitta*) into three parts: *manas, buddhi,* and *ahamkar. Manas* is the recording part of the brain, and it receives impressions and knowledge gathered by the five senses from the outside world. In our modern context, manas would be the resultant formation of neural networks through-out the brain where information is stored. *Manas* accepts all input as fact and makes no judgment as to truthfulness, morality or ethics. In modern jargon, it is what we call the subconscious."

"*Buddhi,* on the other hand, is the judging faculty of the brain. It is logical, and makes moral, ethical, and truthful judgments and decisions. This is what we call the conscious mind."

"The third part, *ahamkar,* is the *ego* which claims these impressions are its own and saves them in the brain as its individual knowledge. 'It's my knowledge and no one else's.'"

"Because the *ego* is tremendously influenced and molded by social norms, I like to think of it as a product of social and cultural hypnosis. For example, unlike the preference of most men in the western world, full-figured women are highly prized and considered beautiful by Samoan men. This is simply cultural hypnosis, and it can be learned or unlearned. In fact, for the 17th-19th centuries, all you need to do is to look at most paintings of women during that period to realize that during those three centuries, full-figured women were considered most favorably in the western world."

Peter

"If I'm honest, I must admit, I've been hypnotized by the 21st century picture of attractive women."

Boda

"I'm not surprised, Peter. It's the usual path of most men. But keep in mind that you can change those things that don't serve you well. Your subconscious is quite susceptible to reprogramming through hypnosis, but better yet, through meditation to higher levels of consciousness."

"However, allow me to continue. Briefly, the mind works something like this. Let's say you're walking through the park on a lovely spring day and you see a beautiful young woman coming towards you. You have seen her here before. *Manas* (your subconscious) would say, 'There's a beautiful young woman I've seen in the park before, approaching me.' *Buddhi* (your conscious mind) decides, 'She's staring at me. She seems to be flirting with me.' *Ahamkar* (your *ego*) might respond, 'I'll bet she would love to meet me.'"

"Patanjali would conclude that in this instance the mind process works this way: 'It is *I* (*Buddhi*) who sees this beautiful woman. It is *I* (*Manas*) who believes she is staring at me and flirting." *Ahamkar* (ego) might conclude, 'Now *I* absolutely know that this woman is attracted to me. This is my own personal knowledge, and therefore I will introduce myself to her when I feel it is the appropriate moment. She will be so happy when I do so.'"

Peter

"I'm still baffled by Patanjali's thinking. I mean more than 2,000 years ago. Really?"

Boda

"You're not the only one. That's why his writings have been studied by scientists and philosophers over the centuries."

Peter

"How does all of this relate to Personal and Cosmic Consciousness?"

Boda

"Patanjali maintains that Personal Consciousness is infinite, and an attribute associated with the individual. He calls it the *Atman*, the word used today in Hindu scriptures. He says the Atman is the real *Self*. It is God within us."

"We often think of the mind as intelligent and conscious, but it's not. It has in fact borrowed its intelligence from the *Atman*, or Personal Consciousness and from Cosmic Consciousness—the latter is called *Brahman* in Hindu philosophy. It is what Buddhists call God *within* and *without* of you. Christians refer to it as God *immanent* and *transcendent* to you."

"Your mind reflects the intelligence and consciousness of Personal Consciousness and Cosmic Consciousness, and therefore appears to be intelligent and conscious. Remember the Akashic Record? That's where all intelligence is coming from, and the amount of this intelligence depends on the functioning of your mind. Remember your black math problems?"

Peter

"Yes, I do remember them—very clearly and happily. I have another question—how important is the structure of the brain in consciousness?"

Boda

"The physical structure of your brain, and therefore your mind is very important. It determines how effectively you can access the intelligence of Personal and Cosmic Consciousness. It functions like a control valve for information from the Akashic Record. An accurate answer to any question you might contemplate resides within Cosmic Consciousness. In principle and in practice for those who are spiritually adept, if you can open the valve to the point of enlightenment, you could answer any question that is answerable. Some questions such as, 'What is the precise nature of Cosmic Consciousness?' are not answerable."

Peter

"What can we do to optimize this process?"

Boda

"The means to achieve that is relaxation, mindfulness and meditation, three of the most powerful tools in our arsenal. Effective practice of relaxation, mindfulness, or meditation can create a truly illumined person, one who is totally calm and at peace, even during challenging times of misery, disease, and strife."

Peter lay back on his blue carpet and looked at the sky.

Peter

"You know, Boda, you've given me a mind full today. I need to think about it. What do you say we call it a day?"

Boda

"Good idea. For next time we meet, now that we have defined the mind and its primary elements, it is important to understand a bit more clearly the three fundamental states—the ego, the conscious mind, and the subconscious mind."

Peter

"That should be fun."

Boda smiled as Peter left to complete his hike as usual.

Dialogue 7
Minding You

"Biology gives you a brain. Life turns it into a mind."
—Jeffrey Eugenides

Peter was anxious for his next meeting with Boda. Some of his teachings on mind, matter, and consciousness were beginning to sink into his own mind, but more dialogue was necessary for him to feel comfortable with what he was learning. How could he use this information to answer those challenging questions he often thinks about?

Boda

"Peter, it looks like you've had a good night's sleep. Are you ready to know about the mind and consciousness in a little more depth?"

Peter

"I hope so. Although I've been intrigued and amazed at what we've discussed so far, some of it has been mindboggling—no pun intended, really."

Boda

"You're on the ball this morning, young man. Okay. Let's start with the ego. Are you fine with that?"

Peter

"Good with me."

Boda

"Great. So, the ego is simply the intense desire of your mind to identify with physical and emotional things, as well as thought forms. It's the basis for all duality, where it silently and cleverly reiterates repeatedly, 'This is me and that's you. This is mine and that's yours. We're different and certainly not connected.' Those affirmations are the epitome of duality. The ego does not want you to recognize that the real you, the *Self* or the I in you, is your Personal Consciousness. And it does not want you to know that duality is an illusion, for in *reality*, as I hope you now understand, all is connected."

Peter

"I'm beginning to understand. But then why do we even need an ego? It seems to have only negative value and doesn't contribute to the evolution of consciousness."

Boda

"It seems that way, doesn't it? But it does have an important role in the evolution of consciousness, and I'll come back to that shortly. For now, I want to emphasize that the ego in effect says, repeatedly, 'Look at me and only me! Look at what I've got and it's all mine! I am my beautiful car, my big expensive house, my super job, my hefty bank accounts, and all my other wonderful and expensive possessions and outward physical accomplishments. Isn't it obvious to you and isn't it impressive?' Such egotistical duality, as it's called, is the basis and prime driving force for our thriving consumer society because we all want and believe we need more stuff to satisfy our ego. As a postscript to one of our prior discussions, it's also a major contributor to climate change."

Peter

"I get it and I'm probably as guilty as the next person. I try to catch myself, but it's difficult—especially when the way this world works is based on competition and acquiring things—expensive things—things we think set us apart from all the others. Sure, we talk a lot about teamwork, but when it comes down to the important things—compensation and getting ahead—let's face it, it's the individual, the me, me, me that counts—we're all butting our heads against each other."

Boda

"I understand. You're not alone in this. The ego identifies with outward things, and in the extreme, this can lead to an obsession with and a compulsion for endless economic growth and diminish our possibilities for spiritual growth. The ego loves having and doing, and cares nothing about being. In fact, it actually fears and resents the act of being because that moves you farther and farther away from doing things or having stuff."

"In the extreme, the ego attributes no value to anything that increases your true quality of life and long-term fulfillment. In this sense, it has sometimes been compared to a cancer cell. It has a blind, voracious appetite for 'more, more, more.' It seeks to proliferate in the organism in which it resides, even to the destruction of that organism and therefore, ironically, to itself. It constantly professes, 'I want to continuously inflate and could care less about what happens to anything or anyone else.'"

"It's not that you should devalue the possessions you have, but when attachment becomes compulsive, obsessive and paralyzing, the ego is in charge and it takes over your actions and your life."

"However, the ego is not evil. It is simply not conscious, which is why it is destroyed upon death. It's not in any way associated with your Personal Consciousness—your soul. Unfortunately, some of us don't realize this until our spirit is about to leave our body."

Peter

"Boy, that's scary. I'd hate to go that way."

Boda

"Most people would agree with you, but some come to that conclusion a bit too late. On this point, I'm reminded of the final scene in a film that many film schools consider one of the best motion pictures ever made—*Citizen Kane*. This 1941 film—written, directed, and acted in by the late and famous Orson Welles—is loosely based in part on the life of American newspaper magnate, William Randolph Hearst, whose name in the film is Charles Foster Kane."

"At the end of his life, as Kane lies on his deathbed, he struggles during his last moments, continuing to mumble incoherently over and over, the word rosebud. No one understands what it means or what he is trying to say. The camera then cuts back to a scene during his childhood and the sleigh that he played with during simple, happy winter days as a young boy. And there on the sleigh is written the manufacturer's name: Rosebud. With all of Kane's accumulated wealth, power, and possessions, the only thing that appeared to matter to him as he was about to die, was a simple happy experience from his childhood."

Peter

"Well then, the big question—how do you control the ego?"

Boda

"There are two things that bring the ego under control. The first is simply recognizing when it is taking over and in effect, catching it. Don't fight back, just observe what is happening. Think Rosebud. The ego is like a naughty child. It hates being caught. That simple recognition begins the process of balancing the impact the ego has on your behavior. In a sense, it leaves immediately and goes into hiding until it can emerge again."

"The second thing that brings the ego under control is suffering. This is the basis for much of Buddha's teachings in his philosophy of the Eight-fold Path.[13] It is also the reason why some people, who undergo a major crisis in their life, often arise from it in an awakened, more conscious state. It can change their life for the better, allowing them to achieve long-term fulfillment and happiness."

Peter

"It seems to me, the best thing to do is to work hard at getting rid of your ego."

Boda

"No, not at all. You just want to keep it under your control. And this is the answer to your earlier question. Ironically, the ego is necessary for our journey to enlightenment. It is by facing up to its power and dissipating its energy by controlling our incessant focus on the out-of-control obsessive thinking of our mind, and moving that focus to the now, namely the present in our life and to universal connectivity, that we achieve lasting true awakening, both here and hereafter."

Peter

"Okay, I think I'm beginning to understand the pros and cons of the ego. What about the conscious and subconscious minds?"

Boda

"There are a huge number of volumes addressing the nature of the conscious and non-conscious or unconscious mind. The latter is often referred to as the subconscious. However, many psychiatrists, starting with Sigmund Freud, believed it is not a proper scientific term. Others, including philosophers Jean-Paul Sartre and Erich Fromm, debated whether such a well-defined entity exists separately from the conscious mind, but I assure you, it does. I think the presence of a subconscious is now broadly accepted by the global psychiatry community."

"For our purposes, we only need to understand that in addition to the ego, there are two important separate functions interacting with our Personal Consciousness— the conscious mind and the subconscious mind. These two functions are considered major parts of human awareness."

Peter

So, what do these two minds do?

Boda

"Your subconscious absorbs everything that you experience with your five senses, as well as any information that your conscious mind cannot at any given moment process and make meaningful and logical sense of. Your conscious mind is often not capable of absorbing disconnected information, as it could lead to a heavy overload, confusion and mental chaos. Thus, the subconscious, which has huge capacity, stores this information until your conscious mind needs it and can make logical sense of it.[14]"

"Without any doubt, the subconscious is the most important part of your mind. It is the part of your mind which functions below self-awareness. It manifests your circumstances, and most importantly, it is receptive to guidance from your conscious mind. One way of looking at this is *the subconscious mind is what you truly are, and the conscious mind is what you know.*"

Peter

"It's weird to think that much of what we are is acquired subconsciously."

Boda

"It is, but this part of your brain can have great value in getting you what you want. The subconscious plays an important role in manifesting your desires into your life. In this respect, it's important to assume that which you want to bring into your life is already there until your conscious thoughts become your subconscious belief. Whatever you suggest with conviction to your subconscious is the law that guides your actions. It also guides the actions of others through the force of Collective Consciousness. This is how it brings forth your desired manifestations. Your subconscious is never objective or judgmental concerning thoughts sent by your consciousness. Right or wrong, it accepts them as fact."

"The subconscious reasons deductively and is never concerned about the morality, ethics, truth or fallacy of the premises that are imprinted upon it. It proceeds on the assumption that those premises or instructions it receives from your conscious mind are correct, and it seeks results and actions that are consistent with them."

Peter

"Boy, that's kind of scary. The subconscious seems to me like a form of hypnosis."

Boda

"Excellent. Like meditation, hypnosis is an altered state of consciousness, and similarly, it can program your subconscious in a manner such that your conscious mind is completely unaware. In hypnotism, your conscious mind is put to sleep and your subconscious powers are openly exposed so that they may be directly manipulated by suggestion."

"Properly administered, hypnosis is a powerful tool to instruct and manage the subconscious. A good hypnotist can hypnotize even a highly skeptical person and suggest he or she will cluck like a chicken when a certain word is mentioned. The hypnotist then 'awakens' the person from the hypnotic trance, and he or she enthusiastically cackles like a chicken upon the mention of the designated word. This entertaining behavior can then subsequently be erased by the hypnotist."

Peter

"Has anyone ever combined hypnosis with meditation?"

Boda

"Good question. Although some researchers have experimented with the concept, to my knowledge, no one has ever formally and seriously merged the practice of meditation with hypnosis. However, it may be a useful way to help those who find it difficult to focus enough to enter the meditative state."

"It's critical to understand the relationship between the conscious and subconscious minds. The reason is that the universe and everything in it, including you and me as physical beings, are manifested by consciousness; and in this realm, the subconscious can be a valuable tool. Remember, consciousness is the true reality, not what you perceive with your five senses."

Peter

"That's beginning to come through, loud and clear."

Boda

"I'm pleased to hear that, Peter. In fact, consciousness is the cause as well as the effect or substance of the entire universe. Your subconscious plays a critical role in creating your life, and if you are to manifest what is important to you, you must become the master of your subconscious."

Peter

"That's interesting because like most people, I have always thought that my conscious mind is what's really in control of all that I do. But I now see that's not the case."

Boda

"Correct. In fact, your understanding and knowledge of what might be called The Law of Consciousness—the mutual interaction and function of the conscious and subconscious—can enable you to accomplish all that you seek or desire to create a fulfilling life. Your conscious mind is personal, selective, and judgmental, while your subconscious is impersonal, unselective, and nonjudgmental. Your conscious mind is the domain of the effect, while your subconscious is the realm of the cause. Your conscious mind generates ideas and concepts and impresses them upon your subconscious. As your subconscious receives these ideas and concepts, it gives form and expression to them—and very important, as I've said—it never makes any judgment about them, whether they are good, bad, moral, immoral, or whatever."

Peter

"Let's see if I got this right. My subconscious never originates ideas or concepts. Instead it accepts as true and correct those ideas or concepts that are brought to it by my conscious mind. Then, my subconscious goes about interacting internally and externally with others with the help of Collective Consciousness to make these ideas and concepts happen. I guess that's why our friend Albert Einstein was fond of saying, 'Imagination is more important than knowledge. Knowledge is limited. Imagination encircles the world.'"[15]

Boda

"Well said, Peter. Through control of your conscious and subconscious mind you have the power and freedom for true creation. Therefore, it is critical to learn how to control your ideas and feelings as they will enter the non-judgmental subconscious and be manifested—for better or for worse."

"For example, if you want to get rid of fear you have when speaking in front of an audience, you don't just say, 'I will develop this capability,' or 'I have this capability.' You must learn how to truly *believe*, and I would say even more powerfully, to *know* you already have this capability. The importance of this concept has been articulated so well by modern day philosopher, Neville Goddard."[16]

"He said, 'All creation occurs in the domain of the subconscious. What you must acquire, then, is a reflective control of the operation of the subconscious, that is, control of your ideas and feelings. Chance or accident are not responsible for the things that happen to you, nor is predestined fate the author of your misfortune. Your subconscious impressions determine the conditions of your world.'"

"He goes on to say even more specifically, 'The subconscious is not selective; it is impersonal and no respecter of persons. The subconscious is not concerned with truth or falsity of your feelings. It always accepts as true that which you feel to be true... Because of this quality of the subconscious there is nothing impossible to man. Whatever the mind of man can conceive and feel as true, the subconscious can and must objectify. Your feelings create the pattern from which your world is fashioned, and a change of feeling is a change of pattern.'"[17]

"So, you see, Peter, in effect, conceiving of an idea or a thought and impressing that idea or thought on your subconscious leads to manifestation of that idea. It always brings you results that are consistent with the premises it receives."

Peter

"From what you're saying, I guess the subconscious is an important part of your mind in making things happen—you know, this whole business of manifestation you speak about."

Boda

"Actually, it's the most important part of your mind. That's why psychiatrists say the conscious mind is what you know, but the subconscious mind is who you are. When we combine this finding with the eternal and infinite consciousness we have discussed previously, we get a fundamental truth which is one of the universal laws of spiritual physics—the cooperative interaction of Cosmic, Collective, and Personal Consciousness is the source of all intelligent activity in the universe. The intimacy, yet separateness of these three elements of consciousness initiates, orchestrates and terminates every physical and spiritual (meaning non-material) event that occurs in the universe. And at the human level, all is created subjectively by the subconscious with no judgment of morality or ethics."

Peter

"One message I get from our discussions is that reality is not what most of us think it is. Consciousness is everything.

And the way in which it works with our mind creates the physical reality we experience. It seems that this law enables us to create whatever we want for a better life. And in a meditative state, where you have a high level of consciousness, you have access to the Akashic Record for the knowledge you need to get what you want."

Boda

"You've got it now. Evolution in both realms, physical and consciousness, is inevitable. And for the first time in our brief history, these evolutionary paths can be affected by conscious choice. I can assure you that free will is and has always been alive and well. You can make that choice, because Personal Consciousness and physical consciousness are for the first time both conscious of themselves."

Peter stared at Boda. Neither said another word. Boda, of course, knew the profound implications of what he had just shared with Peter. And it was rapidly sinking into Peter's clever mind. He turned to Boda.

Peter

Namaste, teacher.

Boda

Namaste, Peter.

Peter smiled and left without another word. He would be back.

Dialogue 8
Life Purpose

"Take care not to listen to anyone who tells you what you can and can't be in life."
–Meg Medina

The international school started classes each year in mid-August and that day was quickly approaching. Peter knew he wouldn't see much of Boda after that—most probably, never again. Boda would likely be returning to Mesopotamia, and Peter would be busy with classes and volleyball.

Over the summer, they had become the best of friends. He would miss his discussions with this most unusual man. Peter had learned a lot from him and already was thinking very differently about his life and, for that matter, about life in general—in ways he had never considered before. There wasn't much time left. He hoped they could cover the remaining big questions that often floated through his mind. Life purpose was high on his list. He headed up the hill again.

Peter

"Boda, I was hoping we could try to cover the remaining questions I raised when we first met. What about finding life's purpose?"

Boda

"That's no problem at all. And life purpose is an excellent choice for today. Make yourself comfortable. To begin my thoughts, I want to share an interesting question with you."

Boda rustled a bit on his red carpet, cleared his throat, smiled and began.

"One of your classic American authors, Mark Twain, once posed a question that's relevant to this topic. He asked, 'What are the two most important days in your life?' Like most people, I'm sure you immediately and accurately guessed the first one as the day you were born. But it's the second day that most people miss. I won't push you for an answer." He paused for a moment and then continued, "Twain said the second most important day is the day you figure out why you were born."

Peter

"You're right. I guessed correctly for the first day. And yes, I confess, I was thinking the day you die was probably the second day. But after hearing Mark Twain's answer, it makes a whole lot of sense. Knowing why you were born— your life purpose—has a tremendous effect on the rest of your life."

Boda

"Absolutely! And don't feel bad about missing the second answer, most people do. So, let's get right to it. You may recall in one our prior dialogues I mentioned a brief definition for both the meaning and the purpose of life."

Peter

"Right. You said the *meaning of life* is to find that special gift or gifts you came into this world with and the *purpose of life* is to share them with others and make this world a better place."

Boda

"Good memory, Peter. Those definitions say it all very concisely. However, after what we have covered this summer, I think you're now ready to explore those ideas in more depth."

Peter

"Great. Knowing my life purpose has been one of the big questions I wrestled with before we met. And honestly, I continue to think about it a lot, especially as I think about college and what will I do for a career?"

Boda

"Okay—first I'll summarize in a bit more detail what a life purpose is, and then we can talk about how you can find it and what you can do with it. There's actually a specific approach on how to find and then use it to achieve long-term fulfillment and happiness."

Peter

"Perfect."

Boda

"I can promise you, if you truly understand your purpose and pursue it, you will not only find happiness and fulfillment, you will make a positive difference in the lives of those people around you, and for that matter, in the world. To get to this point, you must find that special part of your body, mind, and spirit that distinguishes you from others in your professional and/or personal circles—that unique something which you are not only good at, but also gives you sheer pleasure and has the potential to generate value for both you and the world. It's really part of what makes you . . . well—you."

Peter

"That sounds to me like an all-around win. Are you telling me that everyone has a purpose? And if so, does everyone find it, and if not, why? What happens then?"

Boda

"Whoa—slow down, my friend. We'll get to each of those points. Let's start with this—that something you're good at and love to do is called your essence. And yes, everyone is born with one or more such gifts that make up their essence. As I said, it's part of who you truly are. The alchemists called it the fifth element, or your quintessence. It's the real you, not what you or someone else *thinks* you are or should be, but—deep down—what you have always wanted to be—what you were born and meant to be!"

"Most of us know what it is when we're young, but for many of us, the machinations and rapid momentum of our modern technological world are a distraction and often push us on to another track—one that can be unsatisfying and unproductive. Your parents always wanted you to be a doctor, or a lawyer, or to fall in line and work in the family business. And so, you did. But is that what you really wanted to do? So now you find yourself saying something like, 'Can't wait until I retire, then I can do what I really want and like to do!' There is a wonderful and prescient comment by Glenda Burgess in her book, *The Geography of Love*— 'What you dream of yourself at age fourteen reflects your purest wish.'"[18]

"Or possibly there is a distracting, overbearing recording that has echoed over and over in your mind since childhood, something like, 'Everyone tells me that a degree in business is the best way to a high-paying job and financial freedom. And for goodness sake, forget about your deep interest and special capabilities in the arts or music or sports. Do you want to be a pauper all your life?' Many people end up pursuing 'practical' professions, not ones that are based on their innate strengths, capabilities, and deep interests. Here, practical equates to a means to money, status, and power. This has been the definition of a practical profession for more than three centuries—ever since the start of the Industrial Revolution."

Peter

"So, I guess many people either don't recognize or don't accept their personal strengths and as a result, they don't find their life purpose. How unfortunate—for them and for the world."

Boda

"You're absolutely right. Is it any wonder then that recent studies show that only 80 percent of employees are happy with their jobs?[19] And as for so-called 'successful' business people, less than 20 percent have truly satisfying marriages and close relationships.[20] The point is that more often than not, your true interests and capabilities, if properly pursued, have the highest probability of providing personal satisfaction and also in making a positive impact on the world around you—and more often than not, even bringing you a tidy financial return."

Peter

"That's amazing. I would think would be a big motivator—making good money by doing what you're good at and love to do, and helping the world, as well. I can't understand why more people don't pursue their dream and do what they're good at."

Boda

"It's primarily because they don't take the time to go through the process to get them there, and sometimes, without any thought at all, they may not believe the skill set they have can make a difference. First, it's important to take the time to identify your skills. And you must do this without having in mind a specific a profession or purpose. In doing this, you can identify your essence, those special skills or capabilities you came in this world with. They can be divided into hard skills and soft skills."

Peter

"What's the difference between hard and soft and can you give me a few examples?"

Boda

"Sure. Hard skills might include your natural capabilities in areas such as the arts, music, dance, sports, math, science, writing, computers, mechanics, analytics, languages, etc. Soft skills could include special capabilities in leadership, courageousness, resiliency, team playing, self-awareness, flexibility, storytelling, communication, etc."

Peter

"It sounds to me like hard skills are specific things you can do well, and soft skills are more like how you do things really well. Are the hard skills more important than the soft ones?"

Boda

"Don't be misled, soft skills are as important as hard skills, in some instances, even more so. But then comes the challenging part, and that's when many people give up. You must work patiently and diligently to discover a need in the world that would benefit by application of your skills. Don't lose heart, or as you would say, hang in there. When you hit upon an important need in the world that would benefit, you have found your purpose for that stage of your life. Although your purpose may change at various stages of your life, your essence does not. That's who you are. It's your very core, part of your soul."

Peter

"That sounds exciting to me. I can see how it can change your life."

Boda

"It does and here's why. You will find that this insight leads to intense passion. You become tremendously excited about your idea. This ignites high levels of physical and emotional energy, which unleashes unusual creativity. You will be able to solve problems you never thought possible for you to resolve. This is because you now are in a mental state where there is rapid connection between the left and right sides of your brain. This enables you to simultaneously draw on both sharp analytical and amazing intuitive skills. The result is almost always innovation—you can see a positive impact in the world. And when you follow through, this eventually provides a reward. It may be financial, emotional, psychological, spiritual, or some combination of all four. You cannot escape a deep sense of gratefulness, which is always the source of lasting happiness. You have discovered and navigated what can be called the path to fulfillment. In summary form, it looks something like this."—Boda pulled out a pencil and piece of paper from his backpack and quickly scribbled the following word equation.

Essence→ Need → Purpose→ Passion →
Energy→ Creativity → Innovation → Reward →
Gratefulness → HAPPINESS & FULLFILMENT

But, Peter, please don't take this equation too literally. I show it to you because of your mathematical inclinations. It's just a way to show you the overall flow of things. In some instances, there will be feedback loops that reinforce this process. For example, after having discovered an exciting need and purpose, your passion, energy, creativity, and innovation may inspire you to discover an even greater need, and the flow will then proceed again as shown in this equation towards happiness and fulfillment. You get the idea?

Peter

"I do. Now that I see the complete picture, it all makes sense. But like all good things, it requires some work. No free lunch."

Boda

"You're right. The point is that if you earnestly uncover and follow your purpose and build your life around it, you are much more capable of creating a successful life and the enriched relationships that flow from that success. You will also discover that this new-found purpose and passion unfolds creative approaches to tough challenges, even for the most ordinary pursuits and because of that, it can provide significant emotional and financial rewards."

Peter

"This is sounding better and better to me. Why would people not do this, since a life of purpose eventually leads to a successful life for you and probably lots of benefits to many people around you? And if you haven't done this, is it ever too late to try?"

Boda

"In fact, it is nearly impossible to have a truly successful life without a purpose that, if truth be told, is what your soul yearns for in the first place. And for those who have lost sight of their purpose in life, have no fear—you can find or recapture it. It's never too late to change—under almost any set of circumstances. Harland Sanders was 65 years old when he founded the multibillion-dollar KFC enterprise, and his prime competitor, Ray Kroc founded McDonalds at age 56. Please don't think I'm promoting fast, packaged food. I'm not. I'm just making the point."

"It does, however, require courage, commitment and an internal sense that you will eventually uncover a strategy that will help you make the transition, successfully. The great thing about this process is that once you identify your life purpose, the passion created just in that step alone, provides a lot of the motivation, courage, and energy you'll need to make the necessary changes and get to gratefulness, fulfillment and happiness."

Peter

"I know what you mean. I've sometimes gone into a shop to buy something and met a grumpy person who is clearly unhappy at what they're doing. I felt like telling them, 'Why don't you get a life?' I now realize that's an unkind thought. For whatever reason, they haven't yet found their life purpose. I guess what I should be thinking is, 'Hey, why don't you find what you love, so you can love what you do.'"

Boda

"Well said, Peter. You know, Paulo Coelho, author of *The Alchemist,* tells us in this wonderfully incisive fable that all of us know what our essence is when we're quite young. But the ways of the world have the effect of dulling our senses. By the time we are adults, we often have either forgotten what that special gift is, or we have been talked out of it by misguided family members or friends, who sincerely believed they had our best interest in mind. You don't think in these terms when you are a youngster, but that special skill is there, and you can discover it in the strangest and most unexpected way."

"Never before has it been so important to understand and follow your purpose. It can help heal the world. I think we are at a critical time in human history, close to a precarious tipping point. We can either fall further into the dark abyss that currently is being created by the challenges that face our global community, or we can transition to a new, exciting, and productive paradigm. This new way of being is embraced by an increasing number of change-makers throughout the world, thinkers at higher levels of consciousness, who recognize what is at stake and want to help create a sustainable humanity where everyone has an opportunity to find happiness and fulfillment."

Peter

"I'm thinking about the discussion we had about climate change. I hope some of those change-makers can help us find a way to deal with that issue."

"I see the path to happiness and fulfillment, and as I look at it, I think it all flows somewhat naturally after you have answered the two most challenging questions—what are those special gifts you were born with, and what are the needs in the world that would benefit from them?"

Boda

"You're right. Say Peter, my legs are getting a bit tired. How about we take a walk and when we return, I have a basket here which contains enough tasty food for a nice picnic. Can you stay for lunch so we can digest what we have learned today?"

Peter

"Sure, but I don't want to take your lunch away from you."

Boda

"Oh, you won't. I knew we would have lunch together."

Peter

"Now, how could you possibly know that? No, wait . . . I know . . . 'been there done that,' right?"

They smiled at each other, as they got up from their respective carpets, rolled them up and packed them neatly next to the picnic basket beneath the undergrowth next to an elderly Linden tree. Peter led the way along the ridge. Both admired nature's beauty in the valley below, not saying very much. They didn't have to. It would all eventually be said before summer's end.

DIALOGUE 9
FINDING IT

*"You have succeeded in discovering your Personal
Legend... It's what you have always wanted to
accomplish... Everyone, when they are young,
knows what their Personal Legend is."*21
—**Paulo Coelho**

Peter arrived at the usual meeting spot early, but Boda
was nowhere to be found. He decided to walk towards
the top of the ridge to see if for some reason he had gone
to the hunting blind. He turned but hadn't taken but a few
steps when he heard a voice from behind him.

Boda

"Where are you going?"

Peter

"Oh, morning Boda. I was a bit early today and wondered
if you were here yet. Hey! Where did you come from, anyway? I mean, seconds ago you weren't here, sitting on your
red carpet. Where in the world? I mean, how did you . . .?

Boda

"I just kind of popped in."

Peter

"Yeah. I realize that. But, from where and how?"

Boda

"Oh, from here, there and everywhere. You know—the usual."

Peter

Peter just smiled. "Yeah, right." He decided not to pursue it any further. Gathering his thoughts in a different direction, he said, "You know, I appreciate your idea of following that word equation of yours to happiness and fulfillment. I was wondering if you could give me some specific points on how to work my way through the process, especially finding my essence and life purpose. That looks like the tough part. From what you've already said, the other steps seem like they'll be easier once that's done."

Boda

"Sure, that's not a problem. Sorry for reiterating this, but it's quite important to keep it in mind. Like anyone else, you are eminently capable of finding your essence, that special part of your body, mind, and spirit that distinguishes you from others—that unique something which gives you sheer pleasure and has the potential to create great value for both you and the world. It's what you were born to be. As I've said before, when you connect it to an important need in the world, you will have discovered your purpose and that will give you passion as you've never experienced before. And you're right, the hard part is identifying your essence and a specific and relevant need in the world, and then connecting these two together. Then you will have found your life purpose for that period of your life. The rest does flow quite naturally."

Peter

"That all sounds great, but can you give me something more specific to do that can make this all happen?"

Boda

"Oh Peter, I love your impatience—sometimes—that is. To your request, in a few moments, I will share four questions with you that if answered truthfully can lead to your essence, purpose and passion. I want to caution you upfront that they will seem like simple questions, but they will require some deep thought on your part to get answers that will make a difference, in fact, that will change your life."

Peter

"Okay, I'm eager and ready—what are the four questions?"

Boda

Smiling and certainly joking, Boda remarked, "I said sometimes I love your impatience. Before the questions, I want to make a few remarks about the process."

Peter

"Okay, okay. Sorry. I guess you can see how anxious I am to get started."

Boda

Boda smiled. "So, to achieve best results with this inquiry requires a concerted, consistent, and focused effort, but the outcome is more than worth the effort. After all, it is *your* life. When contemplating these questions you might sit comfortably in a quiet place, for example, in the wilds of nature such as this beautiful forest, at the seaside, on a mountain, or perhaps simply in a quiet place at your home—wherever you feel safe, quiet, meditative, and readily inspired. If you meditate daily, you will find the process to be significantly easier, especially if you think about these questions just before meditation and letting them percolate within your subconscious. By now, you should be well practiced in the process of meditation."

Peter

"I'm certainly not an expert, but I've come a long way this summer with all of the help you've given me on how to get to higher states of consciousness. I'm getting pretty good at it and can see the difference. I can solve tough problems—not just math—more easily, I sleep much better and I feel more inspired and healthier. My volleyball game has even improved—I love it. It's changed my life and I'm grateful to you."

Boda

"Thank you, Peter. I'm happy for you. I want to emphasize that in asking yourself these four questions you must be totally honest with your responses, and not provide answers your parents, loved ones, or teachers might like to hear. Don't be frustrated if the answers don't come immediately—they almost never do—but in time you will move into the answers. Be patient, be tenacious and be blatantly truthful. The more often you practice this meditative process, the sooner you will have your answers. Followed diligently and with commitment, this process always works."

"The reason I emphasize mediation is because the answers to these four questions must come from deep within your soul. There's no room for modesty in this undertaking. Don't worry about being egocentric. You are only speaking to you. And besides, you're looking for that part of you which is exciting and probably more adept than many of those around you. Don't be shy!"

Peter

"Who, me? Shy? You must be kidding!"

Boda

"Sorry, you're right. I shouldn't worry about you on that point. However, there is another important one. I encourage you not to focus on making lots of money. It could easily confuse the process. Sure, as Abraham Maslow[22] and Viktor Frankl[23] keenly recognized, you need enough money to satisfy your basic needs in life, but anything after that is just a measure of your professional progress in western culture. Besides, there are lots of examples which show that financial success often follows from the pursuit of purpose."

Peter

"To zero in on what might be my true essence—what you've called hard and soft skills, how do I start?"

Boda

"I suggest you think back to your early youth as well as your current stage in life and focus on those things that interest you above all others. It is likely these skills showed up early on and captured your interest as a youngster. When people are young—somewhere between the ages of five and fifteen—these skills may be expressed in an unusual manner. But I can tell you that in most cases, early in their youth, most people know exactly what they are good at. Although at that point they may not be mature enough to articulate it, they have a good sense of the future areas of professional pursuit that will be best for them and for the world."

Peter

"I guess that's right. In elementary school, I was taking things apart and putting them back together. I liked doing puzzles, especially those that had math associated with them. If I think back to that time, I'm sure I dreamed, as I do now, of doing something in the area of science and technology."

Boda

"Great. To support what you're saying, I can tell you that studies have shown that the prime reason for this behavior at an early age is that children in this age range want essentially two important things in their life.[24] First, they want to impress their friends, and second, they want to feel good about themselves through their innate drive for high self-esteem. The best way for them to accomplish these objectives is to do what they are passionate about and what they are good at. Also, at this stage in their life they are not distracted by pursuits that promise loads of money or power and prestige. They want their peers to like them, and they want to love what they do. That's it."

"So, for example, mechanically-adept children, as you were as a toddler, impress their friends by what they can fix and build. Artistically clever children wow themselves and others with their skills in the arts, budding super athletes outperform their competition on the playing field, and so on. Nearly all children in this age range understand what they're good at and what they like to do. And they're not distracted by how to turn their skills into a money-making profession."

"Also, there are lots of options for various skills. Being artistically adept and inclined doesn't necessarily mean the child is destined to become a Picasso or a Rembrandt. He or she might express their artistic passions in a different way, perhaps as an architect or an art critic, or a commercial designer. Similarly, a child competent in sports might be destined to be a coach, a sports agent or possibly open a sporting goods store. The range of possibilities is greater than just one possibility."

Peter

"I'm not sure many people think that way. Most parents want their kids to become independent and self-sufficient.

To them this means get a great education, a high-paying job with lots of possibilities for growth and promotions."

Boda

"There's nothing wrong with that as a general direction. But sometimes, their children find themselves in professions that provide lots of money, but which stir no passion in their soul. I would say to them, if you are not happy with the current state of affairs in your business life, your answers to the five questions may not have anything to do with what you studied in school or what you do in your current job. Just because external influences drove you to become, for example, a lawyer or a banker, doesn't mean you must continue working at that profession for the rest of your life. After being in one position for some years, making a change always looks more serious, risky and challenging than it turns out to be. My counsel to them is don't talk yourself out of trying. Don't get stuck for the rest of your life."

Peter

"It's kind of scary to think someone would spend a large part of their life doing something they're not happy at."

Boda

"It is, Peter. But it happens—unfortunately, too often."

"But now, for those four questions. Answers to the first three questions can help you discover your essence—*1. What are my unique hard and soft skills? 2. What do I love to do, so much so that time passes incredibly quickly when I'm doing it? 3. What work could I do that I would not consider work?* For the first two questions, don't think about making money or any specific profession. For question three, of course, you must consider a profession—but not money."

"Question four—*What challenges do I see in the world, which if addressed using my skills, would be exciting opportunities for me and could provide value to the world and satisfaction to me?*"

"Answers to these questions can uncover an important need in this world and show you how to specifically put this information together to have an admirable life purpose and the passion you so well deserve."

Peter

"I see the point you made earlier—these are simple questions alright, but will require some work to answer truthfully, completely and creatively, so that I can find my purpose and passion."

Boda

"Exactly. But, as I said, it's worth the effort. In fact, it's unfortunate how many people underestimate their innate power and potential to make this a better world and in the process to blossom in personal fulfillment beyond their wildest dreams. Once you get a taste of the progress you can make in this purposeful journey, you will not want to ever turn back. You will feel a deep sense of exhilaration—high levels of both emotional and physical energy—and you will accomplish much more than the humble goals you had previously set for yourself. You will be well on your way to making this a better world."

"Remember, don't try to live someone else's dream, even if that dream belongs to your parents, a teacher, or a loved one. It can't be done. Dreams are person-specific. They can't be borrowed from someone else. Besides, as impossible as it may seem, it requires much less effort to follow your own purpose and passion than to become an unhappy prisoner trying to live someone else's dream."

Peter had learned a lot during this dialogue. So much so, that it would take some time to digest and move forward. But he had a pretty good idea which direction he'd be going.

Dialogue 10
Lasting Happiness

"Happiness is not something readymade.
It comes from your own actions."

—Dalai Lama XIV

It was the last day Peter and Boda would meet at what had become their place, at the top of the ridge overlooking the Nebušice Valley. Classes at the International School of Prague would begin the next day. Discussions with Boda had been a most incredible and unexpected experience for Peter—something he would never forget. Although he was looking forward to their usual morning dialogue, he was more than troubled by Boda's impending departure. How could he ever repay Boda for what he had taught him over the summer? He couldn't—it was priceless.

Peter approached Boda at their usual meeting spot high on the ridge. Although both were smiling, Boda could sense the sadness in Peter's eyes and the heaviness in his heart.

Boda

"Peter, why so glum?"

Peter

"I'm sure you know we're unlikely to see each other again. This has been the most amazing summer. I'm gonna miss our dialogues and being with you.

Boda

"Thank you for your kind words. It may be true on the physical plane, but not on the spiritual plane. After what we've done together this summer, our souls are intertwined, now and forever. When you need me, just as you meditate to touch the Akashic Record, you can do the same to touch my soul. I'll be there in spirit for you—I promise.

Peter

"That's great, but it won't be the same."

Boda

"No, but it will be the way that matters. After all, you now know and appreciate that true reality is not your physical presence. It's your Personal Consciousness, your soul, which is connected to mine through our Collective Consciousness. And because of the close relationship we have built this summer, our Collective Consciousness has even greater overlap."

Peter

"You're right. It's just that I'm still getting used to that. Give me time."

Boda

"You'll have lots of that." Boda looked quizzically at Peter and said, "I have an idea for today's dialogue. I've been thinking that we've covered most of your big questions as well as the spiritual aspects of fulfillment and happiness. Now, I would like to share some thoughts that put happiness and fulfillment in the context of your three-dimensional, five-sense world—after all, that's where you will be living for the rest of your physical life. I think it might be an excellent complement to round out our dialogues. What do you say?"

Peter

Peter was beginning to lose the tension in his brow. With a more authentic smile than earlier, he responded, "Sounds good to me. Let's do it."

Boda

"Okay, then. Let's talk about the *Happiness Syndrome* in this world of yours. The signs are all around you. Every year there are literally hundreds of books and articles published on how to be happy—usually how to get *there* faster, or how to get more of *it*, however you wish to define *there and it*."

"Believe me, this is not a new fad. It goes back thousands of years. Aristotle concluded some 2,400 years ago that more than anything else in life, people seek happiness, usually through beauty, money, or power—and this approach in and of itself—never succeeds.

Peter

"If you watch the news on TV or read the newspapers— which I hardly ever do anymore—it certainly looks like that's the case. And as for self-help books, they're running out of shelf space in most bookstores and libraries."

Boda

"Right you are. Your observations are right on the mark. One point that people often miss is that happiness cannot be achieved directly as a goal. It is always the result of your doing something. Eleanor Roosevelt, wife of one of America's most famous presidents, Franklin Delano Roosevelt, once noted, 'Happiness it's always a by-product.' But then, how does happiness *happen*? What do we have to do to get that byproduct?"

Peter

"I guess that depends on what you mean by happiness."

Boda

"Good point, so let's agree as to what we mean by happiness. Most international dictionaries define happiness as a state of mind characterized by feelings of contentment, love, satisfaction, pleasure or joy. As we have seen before, this certainly happens when you follow the life purpose equation. I think we must also recognize that there is no such thing as constant happiness, except perhaps for a few enlightened saints who spend their lives in meditative bliss. But that's not the path for most people. Their lives are generally lived somewhere between the poles of joy and sorrow, laughter and sighs, achievement and disappointment. The key is how to live a happy life on average. At the end of the day, a week, a month, a year—when you look back, do you feel that deep sense of fulfillment sought by the spirit inside you? Are you happy with what you see? That's the way most people in this world, who are supposedly in the know—psychologists—characterize happiness."

Peter

"That's an interesting description of happiness. I sure hope that someday when I get to that end of the road, I'm happy with what I see when I look back."

Boda

"I have absolutely no doubt you will be. With the questions you raised this summer, at 16 you're probably ahead of where most people are at 60. So then, let's answer the question—what leads to happiness? I think we certainly must live by our personal values, those rules and guidelines ingrained into our consciousness by multiple sources that set the arrow of the compass by which we manage our journey through life. Those values may vary from person to person. However, whatever they are, if you violate any of them, you feel stressed, unsatisfied, and unhappy. But following your basic values is not enough to achieve lasting happiness and contentment. You love math, so as the mathematicians would say, 'It is a necessary but not sufficient condition.'"

Peter

"Super! Are we going to describe happiness with math?"

Boda

"Not exactly. It would take the spirit and fun out of happiness. But we can give it a kind of mathematical twist. I call it the Happiness Formula. Let me explain."

"The pioneers of the Positive Psychology movement founded in the U.S. during the early 1990s struggled with the importance of genetics and environmental factors in determining your state of happiness. In particular, they asked questions such as, 'Are you born with a certain level of happiness or unhappiness? Is there anything you can control to lead to a happier life?' As biologists uncovered the details of the human genome, a more complete understanding of the contributions of nurture and nature began to unfold."[25]

Peter

"In our biology class, we read about this and the effects of epigenetics. But I wasn't sure how much of a contribution genetics really makes."

Boda

"It now appears that your genes have a significant impact on your innate set point for happiness. If you have happy parents, it's quite likely you too will have a high happiness set point. And of course, the converse is true, as well. However, genes are often sensitive to environmental conditions. Furthermore, scientists have found that you can have a significant impact on your state of happiness by addressing the conditions of your life and by what you do with them."

Peter

"I'm not sure I get your point."

Boda

Okay, I understand, but I bet you will get it now, because here comes the math—kind of."

Peter

"Great!"

Boda

"Okay. All of this has been somewhat quantified in the following equation developed by Martin Seligman, a founder of the Positive Psychology movement.[26]

$$H = S + C + V$$

Here, **H** is the level of happiness that you experience. **S** is your genetic set point. **C** is the environmental conditions of your life and **V** your voluntary activities, i.e., what you do with your life. So, the challenge then, since **S** is fixed at birth, is to see what you can do to increase **C** and **V**. Although the relative contributions of **S**, **C** and **V** to happiness can be argued, most psychologists would say that for a normal healthy person the relative contributing weights are approximately: **S** = 40 percent; **C** = 20 percent; and **V** =

40 percent. Therefore, beyond choosing the right parents, your primary potential impact is on **C** and **V**, and it is quite significant—about 60 percent."

Peter

"How can I affect **C** and **V**? What do I have to do?"

Boda

"As for **C**, there are several factors that have been found to contribute and which, if addressed can have a positive impact.[27] The first, believe it or not, is *noise level.* Research has shown that people who must adapt continuously to high levels of noise, find it difficult to do so and this has a diminishing effect on their level of happiness. It's difficult to be happy when you're constantly annoyed. Talk to people who live under an elevated train system."[28]

"In your modern connected world, long-distance commuting also has a negative impact on happiness. In the New York City metropolitan area, it is not uncommon for some people who live on Long Island to travel to work two hours each way in heavy traffic. Research shows that those who do travel extended distances to work exhibit significant stress levels on the job and a diminished state of happiness."[29]

Peter

"I would never have guessed that noise and long-distance commuting would have anything to do with happiness. But, two years ago, my mom decided to completely renovate our home. We rented and moved into an apartment in the center of Prague. After living in this lush quiet Nebušice Valley, the one-hour commute by bus and subway was a real pain. And, wow! The noise level in the Old Town, where we had our apartment was crazy—garbage trucks, delivery vans, drunks yelling at four o'clock in morning. I was a wreck by the time I got to school and when I finally arrived home in the evening. I wouldn't want to do that again."

Boda

"You got to do the experiment, firsthand. Looks like the scientific findings were right on target."

"Another factor which decreases your level off happiness is lack of control. Scientists have demonstrated that changing an institution's environment to increase a sense of personal control among its occupants, such as for patients in a hospital, students in school, or workers on the assembly line, was one of the most effective ways to increase their sense of engagement, energy level and happiness.[30]"

"In one experimental program, two floors of patients in a nursing home were studied. On one floor, patients could choose flowers and plants for their room, care for the plants, and choose a specific movie night each week as well as the movie they wanted to see. On a separate floor, the nurses did all this for the patients. This minor manipulation had significant effects."

"On the floor with increased personal control, patients were happier, more active, and more alert, as rated by the doctors and nurses, and these benefits were still observed even after 18 months. Furthermore, during these subsequent 18 months, the patients with greater control amazingly had statistically significantly better health and half as many deaths—15 percent versus 30 percent.[31] Although the scientists attributed the differences observed for both groups to control, I think a second factor was at work as well. And that factor is purpose. The responsibility for taking care of the flowers and choosing a movie each week also gave these elderly people a sense of purpose."

Peter

"That seems like such a simple change. Those results are amazing."

Boda

"Exactly. Now to complete the story, there are two remaining factors in the **C** component of the *Happiness Equation*. One is shame. People who remove any physical, emotional, or intellectual trait that is responsible for their feeling self-conscious always increase their level of happiness. A large percentage of plastic surgery is marketed to these kinds of patients."[32]

"Finally, and surely not surprising, the final factor that is controllable in the **C** component of the Happiness Equation is relationships. This factor may well trump all the other components of **C** in the equation. As expected, good relationships make people happy, and happy people enjoy more and better relationships than unhappy people."[33]

Peter

"Boda, that's all amazing and some of it quite surprising. Now as I recall from how we started this dialogue, and as the mathematicians would say, there's one variable left, right?"

Boda

"Right you are. Once **S** is fixed by the genetic code and **C** is addressed as best it can be, that leaves only **V**, the most significant factor after **S** to control your happiness. If you are in balance with respect to your basic personal values, I think the fundamental remaining requirement for optimal happiness is that you continuously pursue your sense of purpose, your *raison d'être*, as the French would say. And this means applying your personal essence to create value for both the world and for you. As we discussed a couple of weeks ago, each of us is born with an essence, that fundamental capability or skill that differentiates you from others in your social and professional circles. And when you find that special piece of you and apply it in whatever you do to make the world a better place, it generates passion—an incredible force that evaporates fear, unleashes creativity, and has been known to change the world."

Peter

"From what I've learned from you this summer, I'd say purpose is the most important factor for creating happiness and fulfillment. I wouldn't be surprised that if your passion is strong enough from finding your purpose, then purpose might surpass the other factors, including genetics."

Boda

"I agree with you. And as you can see, finding purpose and passion is something anyone can do if they're willing to work at it—which means—in principle, anyone can find happiness. It's just that some of us must fight harder against the ways of our world to do this. But it absolutely can be done."

Peter

"In terms of people having to fight harder, you mentioned previously that sometimes a person may choose a professional direction that provides them with purpose and passion but isn't supported by friends and family. Why would they not be supportive?"

Boda

"Because in many instances, they honestly and wholeheartedly believe that the two elements that clearly define success are wealth and power. That's how they've been conditioned all their lives. It's not that money and recognition are unimportant—they are to a certain point. It's that there is a third and much more important element—and as you have now discovered that most definitely is your life purpose.

Daily, there are stories in the media about people who have wealth and recognition and yet appear to be unhappy. How many people have you met who have a true sense of purpose and yet are generally unhappy and unfulfilled? I don't think they exist."

Peter

"This must apply a lot to business. You once told me that, on average, only 20 percent of employees are truly happy in their job. I can now see how that could happen if they don't feel a sense of purpose."

Boda

"You're right, which is why it behooves businesses to place their employees in jobs and an environment that are most effective at tapping into their personal essence so that they work with passion and purpose. I admit it's a challenging undertaking but the rewards for both employees and the company are significant. A lack of purpose causes anxiety and people then work inefficiently."

Peter

"It seems so logical. You wonder why it's not happening in every company."

Boda

"Sometimes the most profound ideas have the simplest explanation and because of that simplicity, they seem to fly past people's normal thought process. In fact, you could say that people approach a professional position in one of three ways. The first is simply as a job—primarily to make money. The second is as a career—to achieve their personal goals of advancement and prestige. And the third is as a calling—work that is intrinsically fulfilling because it builds on their personal essence, creates their passion, and contributes to the greater good.

A calling is by far the best means to deep, long-term, lasting happiness and personal fulfillment. It's the kind of thing that changes the world for the better."

Peter

"Great summary. I'm gonna do my best to find my calling. It's nice to see that scientists are trying to understand what makes people happy, both personally and professionally."

Boda

"Peter, there's no doubt in my mind that when the time is right, you will find your calling."

"And as for the science of happiness, Jonathan Haidt is doing great work. He's the author of *The Happiness Hypothesis* and a world leader in the Positive Psychology movement. I like the summary in his book where he states, as Eleanor Roosevelt did, that 'Happiness is not something that you can find or acquire or achieve directly. You must get the conditions right and then wait. Some of those conditions are within you, such as coherence among the parts and levels of your personality. Other conditions require relationships to things beyond you. Just as plants need sun, water, and a good soil to thrive, people need love, work, and a connection to something larger. It is worth striving to get the right relationships between yourself and others, between yourself and work and between yourself and something larger than yourself. If you get these relationships right a sense of purpose and meaning will emerge.'"[34]

"I also advise that you not plan to be wealthy as your personal goal in life. When you do good by producing high-quality work for the greater good, you often do well and achieve wealth, prestige and advancement. Several of the more outstanding examples include—Steve Jobs—Apple; Bill Gates—Microsoft; Sergey Brin & Larry Page—Google;

Anita Roddick—The Body Shop, Arianna Huffington—Huffington Post, Sheryl Sandberg—Facebook and numerous lesser known successful individuals. None of them set out to be wealthy. Each of them found their essence and purpose, and with the passion generated, they set out to make the world a better place."

Peter

"Before we started having these dialogues, just like many of my friends, I thought long-term happiness was elusive and challenging to find. But now I can see that, it's within everyone's reach. And it comes from inside, not outside. All you need to do is be your true self. Embrace your essence, whatever it may be. It's the real you and something to be treasured. Use it to do good in the world and you'll likely do it better than anyone around you, and in doing that, you'll also do well and succeed. You will find lasting happiness."

Boda

Peter, what a wonderful capsule summary. You have been an excellent student.

School started on Thursday. As usual, Peter loaded up with a few Advanced Placement courses, hoping they would help him get into Harvard. Even though he was a straight A student, he was prepared to spend lots of time studying this year—especially for AP-Physics, AP-Chemistry and AP-Math. The physics course covered quantum physics, the chemistry course, organic chemistry, and the math course was a special seminar arranged for Peter and two other gifted students. It focused on linear algebra and topology, both challenging areas of mathematics. It should be an interesting year.

Peter was so busy during the first two days at school he didn't spend much time thinking about Boda. But, on Saturday morning, almost by habit, he got up early and hiked up to their usual meeting spot. He knew Boda wouldn't be there but was compelled to go anyway. All he found were the two ground impressions left by the carpets that they had sat on. He left and decided to complete the usual hike he normally had taken before meeting Boda.

Returning home and after a shower, Peter sat outside in the beautiful garden his mom had created behind their home. It was directly next to the forest. As he sipped on a frosted glass mug of ice-cold lemonade, he reviewed notes he had taken that summer during his dialogues with Boda.

He noticed Boda's suggestion that he read weekly posts by Robert E. Quinn, an authority on how to inspire and achieve positive change in yourself and in the world. It was entitled "Transforming Duty into Love." Three sentences in this post seemed to jump off the page at Peter— "When we do what we are supposed to do because it's our duty, we are *normal.* When we love to do it, we become *extraordinary.* We not only work on the task; the task works on us."[35]

Suddenly, everything Peter had learned from Boda that summer had an even deeper meaning to him. He smiled and knew he would always be in touch with Boda. He was beginning to feel quite extraordinary.

DIALOGUE 11
THE UNIVERSE IN A NUTSHELL

*"The more clearly we can focus our attention
on the wonders and realities
of the universe about us, the less taste
we shall have for destruction."*
— **Rachel Carson**

Peter awoke early Sunday morning. He almost immediately hopped out of bed, walked to the window, and gazed out at the beauty of the forest just past his back yard. He gradually moved deep into thought, replaying many of his dialogues with Boda. *Where— really—was Boda at this moment?*

It wasn't long before he snapped back to his three-dimensional reality. He decided to review two and a half months of notes from his meetings with this amazing man. After a quick breakfast, he went out to a shaded table under a vine-covered trellis in the garden behind his home.

Peter wanted to create a concise summary of the important points that he had learned from Boda. He started to scribble diagrams, wanting to keep his ideas short and to the point.

One big question he had pursued with Boda continued to play in his mind: "What is the purpose of the universe?" After all, it was the basis for all his other questions. If the universe didn't have a purpose, why should anything else have one? Peter jotted down the famous Buddhist mantra:

$$\text{"Sat"} \rightarrow \text{Chit} \rightarrow \text{Ananda"}$$
$$\text{(Existence)} \rightarrow \text{(Consciousness)} \rightarrow \text{(Bliss)}$$

He began to make some notes.

Boda had told him *the existence of all matter and non-matter is eternal.* Although their form may vary from one universe to the next, all matter and non-matter arise and subside. He told Peter this happens by the creation and eventual destruction of each universe back to that incredibly small singularity from which it arose, and which, eventually over billions of years, expands again, forming the next universe. To Peter's amazement, he said, "This is an eternal process leading to increasing evolutionary physical perfection and wholeness for all matter and non-matter, namely Unity Consciousness."

Boda had told him that the sole purpose of the universe is to make Cosmic Consciousness—God, if you wish—continuously and totally aware of Its presence, and to provide for the eternal and infinite growth of Unity Consciousness. Personal Consciousness and Collective Consciousness are the means to make this process happen by accessing the wisdom and knowledge in the Akashic Record, as some might say, the Mind of God.

Love plays an important role in this process—and not simply for moral, ethical or sensual reasons. It's the most powerful force in the universe. It's a force of attraction that makes one plus one much greater than two and makes the *Whole*, much more *Whole*. Perplexed by this concept, Peter had asked how something could possibly be more whole. Boda said, "By eternally increasing Unity Consciousness—making all things, material and spiritual—more as one.

From the natural drive to procreate species to the means to heal material or spiritual entities—whether it is a mountain, a river, an animal, a person, or a soul—when love is applied with compassion, understanding and empathy, no other force can have a more far-reaching, consciousness-enhancing impact.

Love is *the* critical part of the machine that keeps all things moving towards eternal and infinite bliss. It provides the means to continuously and eternally increase the level of consciousness in each successive universe.

Boda told Peter that each successive universe has what he called a cosmic shadow—a precise and accurate memory of what transpired in previous universe. This memory resides in the Akashic Record and is what enables all subsequent matter and non-matter, i.e., consciousness, to evolve eternally to increasingly higher levels.

Peter stopped writing for the longest time and just stared out in focused open-eyed meditation. He put down his pencil on the paper and thought, *could there possibly be anything more important in this amazing cosmos?*

EPILOGUE
ANSWERS TO PETER'S BIG QUESTIONS

"In the deeper reality beyond space and time,
we may be all members of one reality."
—James Jeans

The following is a brief summary of the answers Boda provided to Peter's big questions. The extensive dialogue between these two protagonists provides a more detailed context and, in some cases, a pointed debate concerning his answers.

What is the nature of our universe?

Our universe was born some 13.8 billion years ago in what has been called the Big Bang. It was not an explosion, but rather a very rapid expansion from the smallest imaginable particle called a singularity. That singularity, smaller than the smallest subatomic particle, existed in a field of infinite nothingness, yet contained all the energy and mass that will ever exist in any and all universes.

Expansion of the universe has continued to this very day, but as opposed to what most cosmologists currently maintain, it will not do so *ad infinitum*. Instead, the dark energy and dark matter in the universe will eventually restructure and attain a position in space that exerts maximum gravitational force simultaneously on all the matter in the universe. This will reverse the current expansion into a gradual contraction, eventually forming over billions of years a singularity like the one from which it came. That singularity will subsequently expand again to form a next universe. This process has been happening forever and will continue to do so for eternity. This provides a means to continuously evolve consciousness towards Unity Consciousness. In each succeeding universe, both physical entities and consciousness continue the process of evolution. The properties of the immediately preceding universe have a direct influence on the nature of the new universe. In other words, every universe has a shadow-memory of the last universe and this enables it to make greater strides and progress on both physical and consciousness evolution.

Who am I?
You are an infinite, eternal, and spiritual being having a physical experience. Your five senses and the three parts of your mind—conscious, subconscious and ego—by necessity, mask your knowledge of your spiritual reality. Total knowledge would cause more chaos than the five-sense human mind could bear and manage. This can be overcome to varying degrees by deep meditation. In this state it is possible to access the Akashic Record (*vide infra*), a record of every thought, word, deed, and event that has ever happened, or will happen.

Why am I here?

You are here for two reasons.

1. All living and non-living things—the entire universe—
   are here to enable Cosmic Consciousness—some
   might say God or the mind of God—to be continuously, intimately, and completely aware of Himself,[d]
   as well as the beauty and magnificence of the universe. There has always been and will always be a
   universe. Eternally, there exists the formation and
   eventual destruction of all matter by the inter-
   change of energy and matter from the constant
   level of energy that exists in the cosmos. There has
   never been a single act of creation—meaning the
   formation of something from nothing. Absent the
   universe, God would still be aware of all, but awareness in its totality requires additional sensors and we
   humans are a significant part of those sensors, just
   as our five senses make us aware of the details and
   intricacies of the physical world.

   All living and non-living things have some level
   of consciousness, which connects with Cosmic
   Consciousness and in doing so maintains God's total
   self-awareness as well as His awareness of the magnificence of the universe. A somewhat imperfect
   analogy—if you had only the sense of hearing, someone could tell you about your physical being and

---

[d] The male gender is used here because it is the most common convention for the expression of God. However, Cosmic
Consciousness, i.e., God, is a genderless energy field.

the beauty around you, but total awareness would require your five senses. Eckhart Tolle said it so well, "You are here to enable the divine purpose of the universe to unfold. That is how important you are!"

2. The second reason is that all living and non-living physical things enable the continuous evolution of all consciousness towards Unity Consciousness— physical perfection and wholeness for all matter and non-matter. This is an eternal process. It had no beginning and will have no end.

What is my life purpose?
Your life purpose, as with all human beings, is to recognize your essence, the special gift or gifts that you were born with, and then to identify a positive need in the world and apply your skills to address this need, thereby creating a positive outcome for that need, for yourself, and for the world.

Practiced diligently and properly, this process leads to long term happiness and fulfillment. The detailed path can be summarized as follows:

**Essence→ Need→ Purpose→ Passion→
Energy→ Creativity→ Innovation→ Reward→
Gratefulness, Happiness & Fulfillment**

After identifying your **Essence** and finding an acceptable **Need** on which to apply your skills, you are then able to discover your **Life Purpose** for that point in your life journey. This will evoke a high level of **Passion** and result in incredible levels of **Energy**, both physical and emotional.

This will open a direct and powerful communication between the right and left hemispheres of your brain, simultaneously unleashing unprecedented analytical and intuitive **Creativity**. **Innovation** will abound. You'll solve problems you could never have solved without this process. It will result in **Rewards**—financial, emotional, spiritual, or some combination of all three. You will feel a deep sense of **Gratefulness** within, which results in **Fulfillment** and **Happiness**.

Your **Life Purpose** may change throughout your life. However, although your **Essence** may become more refined over time, it will never change

Experiencing gratefulness is one of the most effective ways of getting in touch with your soul. When you feel gratefulness, your ego steps out of the way, enabling you to enjoy greater love, compassion and understanding. Genuine gratefulness is one of the most powerful ways to invite more goodness into your life. It's basically saying to the universe, "Please bring me more of this." When you connect with this true inner joy, you feel bliss. It is impossible not to.

If you follow this Essence-to-Fulfillment process throughout your life and maintain a sense of life Balance based on your personal and professional values, you can find long-term Fulfillment and Happiness for as long as you live.

What is consciousness?
Consciousness is a spiritual energy field of knowledge and wisdom. It is the true reality or essence of all things, physical and non-physical. In the physical plane, it is most developed

in human beings and in the spiritual plane it is infinitely developed in Cosmic Consciousness.

Throughout the universe, there are three kinds of consciousness—Personal Consciousness, Collective Consciousness, and Cosmic Consciousness. Personal Consciousness is the essence of all physical things—from human beings to the subatomic particles that constitute all matter. Everything throughout the universe is connected. Collective consciousness reflects this overlap and connection. Cosmic Consciousness is the Divine because it has constant and total access to the Akashic Record, which is a complete and accurate record of every thought, word, deed, and event that has ever happened or will happen in the universe. Some refer to the Akashic Record as the *Mind of God*. Paradoxically, all three energy fields of consciousness are separate, yet one. It's the reason that wisdom seekers maintain that God is within you.

Where did I come from?

You did not come from anywhere. As an eternal, infinite spiritual being, you were always here, there, and everywhere. Karma plays a key role in your everlasting life and reality.

Karma is a concept, often misinterpreted as punishment for past unseemly deeds. It is a natural consequence of any thought, word, or deed from you that enters the Akashic Record. As with the laws of Newtonian physics where an equal and opposite reaction follows every action, the laws of spiritual physics analogously predict an equal and opposite reaction for every action on the spiritual plane. Enabling acts, which your personal values maintain are "good or "bad," eventually return to you, respectively, either as a "good" or "bad" reaction, as the case may be—simply a fundamental law of spiritual physics.

Karma is neither bad nor good. Every individual has an opportunity to increase his or her level of consciousness and because of universal connectivity, to increase the level of consciousness of the universe as well. This can only be accomplished by your Personal Consciousness spirit electing to become the soul of a soon-to-be-born individual and during its lifetime to increase its and therefore the universe's karma and level of consciousness. This is strictly voluntary on the part of the spirit or soul, but the eventual rewards in elevated total consciousness can be huge.

How can I find lasting long-term happiness?

Lasting long-term happiness on both the physical and spiritual planes is accomplished by discovering your essence and using it through the Essence-to-Fulfillment process to address a need that makes the world a better place. This is the pursuit of your life purpose.

ABOUT THE AUTHOR

James A. Cusumano (www.JamesCusumano.Com) is chairman and owner of Chateau Mcely (www.chateaumcely.cz/en/homepage), chosen in 2007 by the European Union as the only Green 5-star, castle hotel in Central Europe, and in 2008 by the World Travel Awards as _The World's Leading Green Hotel_. Chateau Mcely offers programs that promote the principles of Inspired and Conscious Leadership, finding your Life Purpose and Long-Term Fulfillment.

He began his career during the 1950s in the field of entertainment as a recording artist. Years later, after a PhD in physical chemistry, business studies at Stanford and a Foreign Fellow of Churchill College at Cambridge University, he joined Exxon as a research scientist and later became their research director for Catalytic Science & Technology.

Dr. Cusumano subsequently cofounded two public companies in Silicon Valley, Catalytica Energy Systems, Inc.—devoted to clean power generation; and Catalytica Pharmaceuticals, Inc., which manufactured drugs via environmentally-benign, low-cost, catalytic technologies. While he was chairman and CEO, Catalytica Pharmaceuticals grew in less than five years, from several employees to more than 2,000 and became greater than a $1 billion enterprise on the NASDAQ stock exchange before being sold.

Subsequent to his work in Silicon Valley and before buying and renovating Chateau Mcely with his wife Inez, Dr. Cusumano returned to entertainment and founded Chateau Wally Films (www.chateauwallyfilms.biz), which produced the feature film *What Matters Most* (2001: www.imdb.com/title/tt0266041), distributed in more than 50 countries.

Dr. Cusumano lives in Prague with his wife, Inez, and their daughter, Julia.

References

1 https://www.britannica.com/biography/Max-Planck.

2 One of the best and clearest descriptions of the Akashic Record is presented by modern day philosopher and scientist, Irvin Laszlo in his book, *Science and the Akashic Field,* Inner Traditions, Rochester, Vermont, 2007.

3 https://history.aip.org/history/exhibits/einstein/inbrief.htm.

4 *NewScientist December 6, 2014, p. 34.*

5 Joshua Howgego, *The Plant Whisperer,* NewScientist, November 24, 2018, pp. 40-41 and https://www.monicagagliano.com/.

6 *Brilliant Green: The Surprising History and Science of Plant Intelligence,* Stefano Mancuso and Alessandra Viola, 2nd edition, Island Press, 2015.

7 Richard Karban, *Plant Sensing and Communication,* 1st edition, University of Chicago Press, 2015.

8 Eckhart Tolle, *A New Earth: Awakening To Your Life's Purpose,* Penguin Books, London, 2005.

9 *How to Know God—The Yoga Aphorisms of Patanjali,*" Translated with commentary by Swami Prabhavananda and Christopher Isherwood, Vedanta Press, Hollywood, CA, 1981.

10 http://www.scientificamerican.com/article/when-does-consciousness-arise/.

[11] James A. Cusumano, *Life Is Beautiful: 12 Universal Rules,* Chapter Three, pp. 41 - 47, 2015.

[12] Op. cit., reference 9.

[13] https://tricycle.org/magazine/noble-eightfold-path/.

[14] http://en.wikipedia.org/wiki/Subconscious.

[15] Quoted in an interview by G.S. Viereck , October 26, 1929. Reprinted in "Glimpses of the Great" (1930).

[16] *Neville Goddard: The Essential Collection; Collected Works by Neville Goddard,* Digital Edition, 2013, Location 2490.

[17] Ibid.

[18] Glenda Burgess, *The Geography of Love: A Memoir* (New York: Broadway Books, 2008) p. 6.

[19] Gary Hamel, Gary Hamel's Management 2.0, "Management's Dirty Little Secret," *Wall Street Journal,* December 16, 2009.

[20] John Cuber and Peggy B. Harrof, http://www.escholarship.org/editions/view?docId=kt9z09q84w&chunk.id=ss2.02&toc.depth=100&toc.id=ss1.35&brand=ucpress.

[21] Paulo Coelho, *The Alchemist,* 10th Anniversary Edition (New York: HarperOne, 1993), Kindle Edition, Location 308.

[22] A.H. Maslow, "A Theory of Human Motivation," *Psychological Review* 50(4), 1943, pp. 370-96.

[23] Viktor Frankl, (I. Lasch, translator) *Man's Search for Meaning: An Introduction to Logotherapy.* (New York: Washington Square Press, 1963. First published in German in 1946.

[24] Clayton Christensen, Curtis W. Johnson and Michael B. Horn, *Disruptive Class, Expanded Edition: How Disruptive Innovation Will Change the Way the World Learns,* 2nd Edition (New York: McGraw-Hill, 2010).

[25] Jonathan Haidt, *"The Happiness Hypothesis—Finding Modern Truth in Ancient Wisdom, " Basic Books, 2006, p. 90ff.*

[26] M. E. P. Seligman, *"Authentic Happiness,"* New York: Free Press, 2002.

[27] Op. cit., Jonathan Haidt, p. 92.

[28] S. Frederick and G. Loewenstein, *Hedonic Adaptation.* In D. Kahneman, E. Diener and N. Schwartz (Eds.) *"Well-being. The Foundations of Hedonic Psychology,* Russell Sage Press, New York, 1999.

[29] M. Koslowsky and A. N. Kluger, *"Commuting Stress,"* Plenum Press, New York, 1995.

[30] Jonathan Haidt and J. Rodin, "Control and efficacy of Interdisciplinary Bridges," *Review of General Psychology* Vol. 3, 317-337, 1999.

[31] J. Rodin and E. Langer, *Journal of Personality and Social Psychology* 35, 897-902 (1977).

[32] Sonja Lyubomirsky, Laura King, and Ed Diener, *"The Benefits of Frequent Positive Affect: Does Happiness Lead to Success?"* Psychological Bulletin 131, No. 6, 2005, pp. 803–855.

[33] H. T. Reis and S. L. Gable, *"Toward a Positive Psychology of Relationships,"* in C. L. M. Keyes and J. Haidt (Eds.), *"Flourishing," Positive Psychology and The Life Well-lived,"* American Psychological Association, Washington, D.C., pp. 129-159.

[34] Op. cit., Jonathan Haidt, p. 238.

[35] https://robertequinn.com/author/robertequinn/.

Made in the USA
Columbia, SC
22 July 2020